Cross-Cultural Dialogues

74 Brief Encounters with Cultural Difference

By Craig Storti

Craig Storti is available as a trainer/consultant in the subjects covered in this book. He can be reached at

e-mail: cstorti@carr.org

Phone: 410-346-7336

Fax: 410-346-7846

Craig Storti is also the author of

Americans at Work: A Guide to the Can-Do People

The Art of Crossing Cultures

The Art of Coming Home

Incident at Bitter Creek

Figuring Foreigners Out: A Practical Guide

Old World/New World: Bridging Cultural Differences - Britain, France, Germany and the U.S.

Cross-Cultural Dialogues

74 Brief Encounters with Cultural Difference

by Craig Storti

INTERCULTURAL PRESS

A Nicholas Brealey Publishing Company

BOSTON • LONDON

First published by Intercultural Press, a Nicholas Brealey Publishing Company, in 1994. For information, contact:

Intercultural Press, Inc.
a division of
Nicholas Brealey Publishing
20 Park Plaza, Suite 1115A
Boston, MA 02116, USA
Tel: 617-523-3801
Fax: 617-523-3708
www.interculturalpress.com

Nicholas Brealey Publishing
3-5 Spafield St.,
Clerkenwell
London, EC1R 4QB, UK
Tel: +44-207-239-0360
Fax: +44-207-239-0370
www.nicholasbrealey.com

Cover design by Studio 3

ISBN-13: 978-1-877864-28-5
ISBN-10: 1-877864-28-5

Printed in the United States of America

11   10   09   08   07   11 12 13 14 15

Library of Congress Cataloging-in-Publication Data

Storti, Craig.
   Cross-cultural dialogues 74 Brief encounters with cultural difference / by Craig Storti.
        p.   cm.
   Includes index.
   ISBN 1-877864-28-5
   1. Intercultural communication. 2. Cross-cultural orientation.
I. Title.

GN345.6.S76   1993
303.48'2—dc20   93-38121
                                                      CIP

For Charlotte,
the Czarina,
with all
my love

Acknowledgments

For the concept of dialogues, I am deeply indebted to Alfred Kraemer who used this technique in work he did for the army in the 1970s.

As for writing and editing, I am once again deeply grateful to David and Kathleen Hoopes who worked their customary wonders with my text. The manuscript arrived on their mountaintop in Vermont as a passable draft—and left as a bona fide book. It was then delivered into the extremely capable hands of Toby Frank and Peggy Pusch who, *mirabile dictu,* made it even better!

As always, I owe deep and lasting gratitude to my wife Charlotte, who has given so much so that I might have the freedom to write.

Table of Contents

The Concept

Every country has its own way of saying things. The important point is that which lies *behind* people's words.

Freya Stark
The Journey's Echo

This book consists of 74 dialogues—brief conversations between an American and a person from another culture. In the course of each of these conversations, the speakers make comments which reveal significant differences in their values and attitudes or in how they view or understand the world around them. The speakers are not *trying* to express these differences—they are in fact quite unaware of them—but the differences manifest themselves all the same as each speaker responds in a completely natural manner to the particular situation. After reading a few dialogues, one begins to wonder if what is "completely natural" to a person from one culture is all that natural to someone from a different culture.

Which is the central lesson of this little book: that when we are merely "being ourselves," acting according to our deepest instincts, human beings reveal fundamental differences in what we all tend to think of as normal behavior. In other words, we learn that much of what we assumed was universal in human behavior is, in fact, peculiar to a particular group or culture. With the inevitable consequence, of course, that whenever we leave that group—to live, work, or do business abroad, for example—or come in contact with people from another group, much of our behavior necessarily becomes suspect.

And that is just what happens, over and over again, in these pages: individuals come face to face with the fact that many of their most cherished instincts don't travel very well, that what is expected and understood in one culture may be shocking and incomprehensible in another. These cultural differences inevitably lead to all manner of misunderstandings, and these misunderstandings, in turn, often result in a wide variety of unpleasant emotional and practical consequences, from hurt feelings and missed opportunities to failed negotiations and lost profits, to anger and hostility, to organized warfare.

By the same token, if we could avoid these misunderstandings, then we would stand a very good chance of sidestepping all the unpleasant consequences they lead to. That, in a nutshell, is the purpose of this book: to alert readers to the misunderstandings lurking in the most common interactions we have with people from other cultures—and to jar us, as a consequence, into being a little less sure of our instincts.

If we look at a sample dialogue, all of this will start to become clearer.

DEAN SMITH: I asked Professor Desai in yesterday to discuss his new course.

MISS SINGH: How was the meeting?

DEAN SMITH: He was very charming. But he avoided the subject of the new course whenever I tried to bring it up.

MISS SINGH: He may be upset that you didn't consult him in advance.

DEAN SMITH: I don't think so. He didn't say anything.

The facts here are simple: Dean Smith, evidently dean of the faculty in a college or university, decided to have one of his faculty members, Professor Desai, teach a new course, apparently without consulting him ahead of time. But when the dean met with Professor Desai to raise the subject, Desai avoided it. Miss Singh, a compatriot of Professor Desai, thinks he must be upset at not being consulted, but the dean feels sure he isn't because the professor "didn't say anything."

But in fact he did say something quite clearly, only Dean Smith didn't hear it. In refusing to discuss the new course, Desai—by the standards of his culture—is signaling his extreme displeasure in a most direct manner. Smith misses the signal because, by his standards, it is too indirect and also because Professor Desai has been his usual charming self. In other words, Smith assumes that someone who is upset is going to say so and that someone who is angry is not going to be charming.

But these are norms—that people will be direct and that angry people won't be charming—and norms, which is where we get our idea of *norm*al behavior, vary from culture to culture. Indeed, in Professor Desai's culture it is very important not to embarrass another person through any kind of overt confrontation. For him to declare outright that he was upset about the new course would make Dean Smith feel very uncomfortable, something that is simply not done (not the norm). Instead, Desai communicates his displeasure indirectly, in this case by not talking about the new course, thus avoiding any kind of unpleasant incident. All the while he maintains the most correct exterior so as not to betray the slightest sign of his wounded feelings, which would only make the dean feel bad if he detected them. It's quite likely, by the way, that Professor Desai has made his feelings very clear to Miss Singh, who is in all likelihood speaking for him (not for herself) when she says to the dean, "He may be upset that you didn't consult him in advance."

Dean Smith and Professor Desai have had a classic cultural misunderstanding, caused by the usual culprit: the fact that each of them assumes the other looks at the world exactly as he or she does. While such misunderstandings can, of course, occur between two people from the same culture, they are much more common between two people from different cultures. And these misunderstandings, as we have noted, lead to all manner of unfortunate consequences which quickly sour—and even poison—relations between people from different cultures.

If we could stop assuming that other people are like us—if we could begin to believe that we don't necessarily understand how foreigners are thinking and that they don't always understand how we are thinking—then we would be well on our way to avoiding cultural misunderstandings and all the problems they give rise to.

Cultural Conditioning

We need to back up here and examine how people come by their behavior and especially why it is we are so intent on attributing our own behavioral norms to complete strangers from the other side of the planet.

We get our norms, our notions of how to behave, from the people around us, and especially from those who raise us. As young children we observe our parents, siblings, and peers and imitate much of what they do and say. Over time we internalize these behaviors, which is to say they become unconscious and instinctive, and we no longer have to think about what to do or say in a given situation; we just know. And what we "know" is what we have taken in from observing the world around us.

But the world that we observe—and the behaviors we internalize—is not entirely the same as the world Mohamed or Mikako observe. Yet they learn their lessons just as well as we do—and come away with a very different notion of how to "be."

In the United States, for example, parents teach their children that it's good to be an individual, that you should be self-reliant ("stand on your own two feet"), that you shouldn't go behind someone's back, and that "where there's a will there's a way." In Morocco, on the other hand, children learn to identify with their primary group (the family). They learn that you can always depend on others (even as they depend on you), that you should never confront another person directly, and that God's will is paramount. With these norms firmly rooted at the level of unconscious instinct, is it any wonder that, when John and Mohamed meet, a cultural incident can't be far behind?

But "teach" is too formal a word to describe the process of cultural conditioning. As a rule, parents don't actually sit down and explain these values to children; most parents aren't even aware they hold them. Rather, these cultural attitudes are merely inherent in the things parents do and say (which they learned from *their* parents), and children, imitating what parents do and say, absorb the values along with the behaviors. This is the reason, incidentally, that people from a particular culture often can't explain when they are asked why they behave in a certain way. "It's just what we do," they say, because they've never thought about the value or assumption behind what they do or even realized there was one.

This is also part of the reason why we so readily project our own norms onto people from other cultures: because these are behaviors we are not aware of ever having learned. And if we didn't learn them, then we must have been born with them. And if *we* were born with them, then so was everyone else. It's not like learning to ride a bicycle; you remember that experience and can therefore imagine that only people who have had that same experience will have learned that particular behavior. But you don't remember learning that "Where there's a will there's a way." So that particular knowledge must come with the species.

Another reason we attribute our norms to perfect strangers is that we've always done so, and it's almost always worked. That is, people have always behaved the way we expected them to in most situations, or at least in enough situations to confirm our view that everyone else is just like us. But of course the reason that most people behave the way we expect them to—that our norms are also their norms—is that they learned the same values and behaviors from their parents that we learned from ours, all of whom grew up in the same cultural environment.

One last reason we expect everyone to behave like us is that we couldn't function if we didn't. The minute you're no longer sure how people are going to behave in a particular situation—

when you start doubting what you know from experience to be true of the world—you will no longer be able to engage success-fully in day-to-day life. In other words, if everything in life were completely unpredictable, if we could not depend on things con-tinuing to happen in more or less the same way they have al-ways happened, we would be paralyzed and unable to act. If we couldn't be sure that other drivers would stop at red lights, that trees would stay rooted to the ground, that airline pilots wanted to live, that passersby wouldn't shoot us—how would we dare leave our homes? We expect people—all people—to think and act the way we do because we have to in order to survive.

The Purpose of the Dialogues

As we have seen, however, it isn't altogether true that all people think and behave the way we do. And for the sake of successful intercultural interaction, the sooner we stop expecting them to, the better. All of which is much easier said than done, for this habit of being right about how people are going to behave—a cornerstone of our being able to function in the world—isn't easy to displace. It takes, in fact, a very strong dose of being wrong about people to bring about the necessary change in at-titude.

This book is the first course of the medicine. After reading these 74 dialogues and being mistaken about other people 74 times in succession, even the casual reader starts to doubt some of his or her instincts. Maybe there are other people who *aren't* exactly like us. And maybe, in dealing with people from other cultures, everything *isn't* exactly as it seems. If you can look this truth in the eye without blinking, you will have taken the first and most important step down the road to cultural sensitivity.

In bringing cultural differences to life, these dialogues make four important points:

1. They show that culture is real, that it actually does turn up in our behavior.

2. They show, therefore, that cultural differences must also be real and that we should try to be aware of them.

3. They present some basic American cultural norms.

4. They present some contrasting cultural norms of selected other cultures.

The reader should read each dialogue and try to figure out either what went wrong or what cultural difference was revealed in the brief exchange. All the dialogues are constructed in such a way that the key to the conversation—the clue to what's not quite right—is contained in the exchange itself. In other words, the reader does not have to know about Arab culture or Chinese culture in order to see what the problem is. You may not know the explanation for what has happened, but you should be able to see what the "mistake" or mistaken assumption was without any additional information. At the same time, we hasten to add that the "mistake" is normally not very apparent. You will have to sniff around for it. Needless to say, if cultural mistakes like these *were* obvious, most of us wouldn't make them.

If you can't figure the dialogue out, try reading it a second time, assuming that nothing is what it seems to be or means what you think it means. Eventually, whether you figure out the dialogue or not, you will want to read the explanatory notes (which follow each section of dialogues) for the observations they offer on American and other cultures.

You will find some repetition of key cultural themes in a number of the dialogues. While the dialogues in each case will present entirely new examples of a given theme, the explanations may sound familiar. We have done this on purpose to make the point (and to offer illustrations of it) that certain profound cultural differences—a respect for rank and status, say, vs. the American ideal of egalitarianism—can manifest themselves in a variety of ways and contexts. And these new contexts, in turn, often reveal additional dimensions of the value or belief under analysis.

Generalizations

The explanations of the dialogues necessarily contain scores of generalizations; one can't talk about cultures without generalizing. But the reader would do well to remember that while generalizations may be accurate about groups, they're never going to be wholly true of individuals. In other words, many of the individual Japanese or Germans you meet may not act at all like the people in these pages.

This doesn't mean we've got our "facts" wrong, but only that in any culture you will always find a broad range of behaviors vis-à-vis a particular characteristic. Take indirectness, for example: you will find some Japanese who are exceedingly indirect, some who are rather indirect (by American standards, that is), and some who are blunt. Or take Americans and the notion of individualism or self-reliance: some Americans are extremely self-reliant, many are rather self-reliant, and some are very dependent. What we mean, then, when we say the Japanese are indirect or the Americans are self-reliant is that this trait seems to *predominate*, to be true of more of the people more of the time than either of the other two extremes. If you think in terms of the bell curve, what we are describing here is the 50 percent of the people who make up the middle of the curve and not the 25 percent who inhabit either end.

Another reason to beware of our generalizations is that while it is only the cultural roots of behavior we are concerned with in these pages, culture is only one of many influences on behavior. Depending on the circumstances, any one or a combination of these other influences—such as social class, gender, age, level and type of education—may be the primary determining factor for any particular example of behavior.

Some American readers may react to the generalizations made about them in these pages and may not even recognize themselves in these dialogues and the explanatory notes. Some possible reasons for this, in addition to those cited above, are: 1) that compared to many cultures, the United States is a very diverse society with striking differences among the various subcultures, which makes generalizing especially tricky and 2) the fact that Americans, because of their well-developed sense of individualism—the much cherished notion of personal uniqueness—are especially put off by generalizations. Indeed, one generalization we can safely make about Americans is that they do not like to be the object of generalizations.

But all of our diversity and individualism notwithstanding, there is an underlying cultural ethos, a shared core of assumptions about people and the world, that most of us would instantly recognize as American (whether we felt it applied to us personally or not). We see it, for example, in many common expressions, such as the above-mentioned "Where there's a will there's a way," and "Stand on your own two feet." And in these:

She puts on airs.
He's pulling rank.
They think they're better than so-and-so.
Don't beat around the bush.
She's all talk (and no action).

It is this core of assumptions that has inspired most of the dialogues in this book.

As we mentioned above, only cultural behavior is discussed in this book—the shared beliefs, values, and actions of a specific group of people—but not all behavior is culturally determined. There is a whole body of behavior that is human or universal that does *not* vary from one group to the next. People in all cultures feed themselves, look after their children, and construct some sort of shelter. Needless to say, when you project universal (as opposed to cultural) norms onto other people, there are no surprises, no misunderstandings, no incidents of the type captured in the dialogues. This is why many of our interactions with people from other cultures are quite successful: because they happen not to involve any behavior that is specifically cultural. In other words, it would be quite wrong for readers of this book to conclude—as they easily might—that anytime two people from two different cultures meet, there will be confusion, misunderstanding, and some sort of unpleasant incident.

At the same time, it's worth noting that it may be because of these human similarities that we so readily project *all* our norms onto strangers. After a few successful interactions, where no cultural difference came into play, can we really be blamed for concluding that foreigners aren't all that different from us? If you combine this phenomenon with the fact that we usually aren't aware of our cultural mistakes—or ever *made* aware of them—this dynamic can lead even someone with extensive experience with foreigners to conclude that cultural differences aren't all they're cracked up to be. "I spent two years in Saudi Arabia," such a person is often heard to say, "and I never had any problems." One is tempted to say the Saudis would be better judges, but one should probably refrain.

Are Americans Really So Boorish?

It's difficult, if not impossible, to read through these dialogues and not get the distinct impression that Americans are an especially thick and insensitive lot who would be better off confined to quarters. Here we are, making mistakes right and left and hardly ever understanding what's going on around us. Are we really so unaware, you'll be asking yourself, so hopelessly unsophisticated and obtuse? If you are an American—and especially if you are a sensitive one—you may become a little irritated, even offended, as you read along.

The answer, of course, is that all the evidence in this book notwithstanding, Americans are not congenital boors or pathologic dummies. While we may be a more naive people than some other cultures that have been around longer, the average American is probably no more obtuse or offensive than any normal person outside his or her home culture.

But you could certainly be excused for reaching just the opposite conclusion on the strength of this book. For the record, then, we want to say that while Americans do come off rather poorly in these pages, that is almost entirely because of the nature and purpose of this book rather than because of anything inherent in the American character. Our objective here, after all, is to show how important it is for Americans to learn about other cultures. The best way to do that, of course, is to depict Americans in a state of *not* knowing about other cultures. Alas, it's almost impossible under these circumstances to end up with a book that is really fair to Americans.

Americans aren't the only people who need to develop cultural awareness; they just happen to be our primary audience, and the dialogues, as a result, tend to be written from an American perspective. But if it makes you, the American reader, feel any better, we hasten to add that a similar book could be written for almost any culture, featuring people from that country in just as dire need of cultural awareness as the Americans depicted herein.

Another point to make here is that in a technical sense neither Americans nor any other nationality are truly insensitive. Rather, each nationality is merely sensitive to different things. Americans, for example, aren't very sensitive to the British value of understatement, but neither are the British very sensitive to the value we place on being direct. People of every culture are equally capable of sensitivity and insensitivity, depending on the context.

The Plan of the Book

Intercultural conversations—hence, cultural misunderstandings—occur wherever people from two different cultures meet and start talking, whether at the checkout stand, the bank, the office, or across the backyard fence. Accordingly, these dialogues have been divided into three categories: Social Settings, The Workplace, and The World of Business. They can occur overseas—to someone living, working, or doing business abroad—or in one's own country when one encounters someone *from* abroad.

The audience for the dialogues, then, is both those people who travel and interact with foreigners on their own turf and those who stay put and deal with foreigners (on and off the job) here in the United States. Indeed, whether or not you have direct contact with foreigners in your day-to-day affairs, there is hardly anyone anymore who can afford not to be aware of how other people around the world feel and think.

2

Social Settings: Dialogues 1-17

She is English; you are Italian. She is accustomed to
one thing, you to another.

E. M. Forster
Where Angels Fear to Tread

We begin with a series of dialogues set in the world at large. We
sometimes feel, when we are relating to people "just as people,"
one to one, with all our titles and roles set aside, that we are
outside the realm of culture, that we can let down our guard
and just "be ourselves." But dialogues don't work like that; they
can occur anywhere at any time so long as the right conditions
come together. And these conditions, quite simply, are a person
raised in one culture talking to a person raised in another.

As for being yourself—alas, that's just the problem, for a
part of every self is deeply rooted in culture. In a world made up
of many cultures, sooner or later—and these days it's usually
sooner—just being yourself is, ipso facto, to be different.

All this doesn't mean, by the way, that there's no pleasure or enjoyment to be had in dealing with people from other cultures, that it's one misstep after another and you might as well accept the fact you'll never figure "foreigners" out and simply get used to perpetually feeling foolish. It's not quite that bad; you'll have many successful interactions with foreigners (and they with you). And those that aren't so successful, where you or the other person becomes confused, misled, or even frustrated, are all potential learning experiences. If you can weather the immediate unpleasantness, you can emerge more aware and sensitive. You may not always be able to figure out what went wrong—what you said that wasn't right or what it was you didn't understand— but at least you'll realize that these interactions aren't always what they seem to be.

1. Dr. Spetsos

MS. SMITH: Do you know Dr. Spetsos?

MRS. KALAS: Yes, we know him very well.

MS. SMITH: I've heard he's an excellent surgeon.

MRS. KALAS: He's a very kind man.

2. Out of Order

NATASHA: Excuse me, but the elevator is out of order.

SHARON: Really? Whom should we talk to?

NATASHA: Talk to?

SHARON: To report it.

NATASHA: I have no idea.

SHARON: Oh, I'm sorry; I thought you lived here too.

NATASHA: But I do.

3.   Class of '97

KAREN: How did you make out at registration?

CARMEN: Quite well. I got into every course I wanted. But one thing confused me.

KAREN: What was that?

CARMEN: They said I was in the class of '97. I don't understand what that means.

KAREN: That's easy. You'll graduate in 1997, four years from now.

CARMEN: But that's just what confused me.

4.   Lucky for Hassan

MS. ANDERSON: Hassan was looking at your paper.

ABDULLAH: He was?

MS. ANDERSON: Yes. He copied some of your answers.

ABDULLAH: Perhaps he didn't know the answers.

MS. ANDERSON: I'm sure he didn't.

ABDULLAH: Then it's lucky he was sitting next to me.

5.   Hannah from Bavaria

DAVID: Good to see you, Otto. How's Mrs. von Klein?

OTTO: She's well, thank you. She had to host a reception at the embassy. What a nice party.

DAVID: There's someone I want you to meet, another German.

OTTO: I see. What's the name?

DAVID: Hannah. She's the mother of that family Kate lived with last year on her high school exchange trip. They have a small farm in Bavaria.

OTTO: I see.

DAVID: Hannah couldn't afford to come to America on her own, of course, so we helped out. We really wanted to meet her. Anyway, now you won't have to speak English all night.

OTTO: I see.

6. *Helping Miss Thomas*

ROBERTO: Miss Thomas! How nice to see you.

MISS THOMAS: How are you, Roberto?

ROBERTO: Fine, fine. Thank you. What can I get for you?

MISS THOMAS: Well, to start with I'd like half a dozen eggs.

ROBERTO: Yes.

MISS THOMAS: And then I'd like 500 grams of butter.

ROBERTO: Yes. Ah, Octavio! Good to see you. Como estas?

OCTAVIO: Bien, gracias. And you?

ROBERTO: Bien. How can I help you?

OCTAVIO: I need some bananas.

ROBERTO: Of course. Rosita! Como estas? I haven't seen you in a long time. How is that little boy of yours?

ROSITA: He's very well.

ROBERTO: What can I do for you?

MISS THOMAS: Roberto, I thought you were helping me.

ROBERTO: But I am helping you, Miss Thomas.

7. No More Pills

MR. BROWN: Did you take the medicine?

MR. PATEL: Yes, I took some last night. Thank you for bringing it.

MR. BROWN: Are you feeling any better?

MR. PATEL: I felt better for a while, but now the pain is back again.

MR. BROWN: I'm sorry. Let me get you some more pills.

MR. PATEL: Thank you, but it's not really necessary.

8. Freelancing

MARGE: Why don't you try more freelancing? Selling to some publications in the United States, for example.

JEREMY: I'd like that, actually. Any help you could give me would be most appreciated.

MARGE: Oh, you don't need me. Just put together a selection of your pieces and send them out.

JEREMY: But I don't know any editors.

MARGE: Doesn't matter. Just send a cover letter explaining you'd like to be their man in London. Or something like that.

JEREMY: Oh, I couldn't do that.

9. Dinner on Wednesday

MR. SOGO: Mr. Collins! Good to hear your voice again. What brings you to Osaka?

MR. COLLINS: Good to hear you too, Sogo-san. I'm here on business with my new company. I'd like to invite you and Ozawa-san to dinner on Wednesday.

MR. SOGO: Thank you very much. I'll tell
          Ozawa-san. Did you hear his good
          news?

MR. COLLINS: No.

MR. SOGO: He's been made president of the
          company.

MR. COLLINS: That's wonderful. Please give him
            my congratulations. I look forward
            to seeing you both on Wednesday.

MR. SOGO: I'm sure Ozawa-san will be very
          pleased to see you again. Where shall
          I tell him to meet you?

10. Neighbors

HELGA: I'm glad you could come by.

TONY: Thanks. Nice place you've got.

HELGA: Let's sit here on the balcony. Can I
       get you something?

TONY: I'll take some juice if you've got it.
      Say, who's that guy in the blue
      Volkswagen?

HELGA: That's my neighbor.

TONY: Really? I've got a car just like that.
      Volkswagen doesn't make them
      anymore; it's really hard to find
      parts. I wonder where he gets his
      serviced? Could you introduce me?

HELGA: Sorry. I don't know his name.

TONY: I thought you said he was your
      neighbor.

HELGA: He is.

11. Near the Family

CATHY: So, Vincenzo, you'll be graduating in May. Congratulations.

VINCENZO: Thank you.

CATHY: Do you have a job lined up?

VINCENZO: Yes. I'll be working for the Banco Central.

CATHY: Good for you. Have you found a place to live yet?

VINCENZO: Actually, the bank's very near my parents' place.

CATHY: That's nice. So you'll be living quite near them.

12. Something Personal

ALAIN: Did you hear? I've been offered a position in Lyons.

DEBORAH: I didn't. Congratulations.

ALAIN: But I don't know if I should take it. It means uprooting my family and moving to the other side of the country.

DEBORAH: You need some advice. Why don't you ask a friend? Pierre, for example.

ALAIN: You mean Gallimart? I don't know; this is personal.

DEBORAH: But you've known him for almost a year.

ALAIN: Yes. That's what I mean.

13. We Miss You

SUSAN: Yang, it's good to see you again.
How do you like your new job?

YANG: It's a very nice place to work. I'm
very happy.

SUSAN: We miss you.

YANG: How is everything at B&G?

SUSAN: You know: the usual. Aren't you glad
you left?

YANG: How are Jan and David?

14. Fathers and Sons

LT. AZIZ: Yes, sometimes the postal service is
very slow.

COL. POST: I finally got a letter from my wife
yesterday. She and the boys are fine.

LT. AZIZ: Oh you have sons! I have sons also,
Colonel Post.

COL. POST: Yes. One is twelve and the other is
nine.

LT. AZIZ: They no doubt will become military
men like yourself.

COL. POST: Who knows? The oldest says he
wants to be a pilot. But you know
how kids are at that age. They're
never sure what they want to do. I'm
sure, though, that when they get
older, they'll make up their minds.

LT. AZIZ: They will?

15. *Humble Beginnings*

HENRI: So your family has been in the textile business for many generations, then, like ours?

RALPH: Actually, not at all. I started out with a retail outlet twenty years ago, and it just took off. We've only had this Paris connection for three years. Needed it when business started booming.

HENRI: I see.

RALPH: My mother still can't get used to the fact that we've done so well and now her son lives and works in Paris.

HENRI: Does she live with you?

RALPH: Oh no. But she came out to visit last year and was bowled over by our house. She still remembers growing up in the hills of South Carolina where they were mighty glad to have a covered outhouse.

HENRI: How charming.

16. *Depression*

CHARLES: Where's Anatoly?

TATYANA: Oh, he decided not to come.

CHARLES: Why not?

TATYANA: He's in one of his moods.

CHARLES: That's too bad. Maybe we should go by and cheer him up.

TATYANA: What for?

CHARLES: I thought you said he was depressed.

TATYANA: He is.

17. Wedding Bells

ALICE: I heard your son is getting married. Congratulations.

FATIMA: Thank you. The wedding will be next spring.

ALICE: How nice for you. How did they meet?

FATIMA: Oh, they haven't actually met yet.

Social Settings: Explanatory Notes

1. Dr. Spetsos

This dialogue captures how two cultures characterize and distinguish individuals. To Ms. Smith, Dr. Spetsos is first and foremost what he does. She instinctively defines or at least categorizes him by his profession. This instinct derives from the value many Americans (though not all) put on work and achievement. We think of ourselves, to a large extent, as what we do, what we have accomplished, and that is how we tend to think of and even judge other people. Not surprisingly, it's also one of the first things we ask when we meet someone (What do you do?), for we believe the answer will in essence tell us who this person is.

In Mrs. Kalas's culture, however, what a person does is not as important—or at least as defining—as his or her personal qualities. It's not that Americans don't care if their surgeons are nice or that Greeks don't care who cuts into them; it's just a matter of degree.

This habit of getting a fix on someone by discovering what he or she does accounts for the exquisite—and singularly American—humiliation of being unemployed. Notice how for many people the great trauma of being out of work isn't so much the financial crisis, but the identity crisis. When someone asks you what you do, you can't very well say: Nothing. For if you do nothing, then you are nobody. Of late, we have even found a way around saying that we're looking for a job; we say, rather, that we are networking. Somehow, it sounds more substantial, more meaningful, you're not a worker, perhaps, but at least you're a networker.

This difference accounts for the rather acute frustration many Americans feel in their first meetings with many Europeans, where the European somehow never gets around to the all-important question: What do you do? He or she never gets around to the question, of course, because the answer won't be especially revealing; what one does in much of Europe is incidental to who one is. But to many Americans, unless you know what I do, how do you know who I am?

2. Out of Order

Sharon can't imagine that someone who lives in a high-rise apartment doesn't know to whom a broken elevator should be reported. But you would only know that, of course, if you were in the habit of reporting such things, which Natasha clearly is not. In her world, elevators break down from time to time, and in due course they are fixed. Meanwhile, one walks.

By and large, Americans are doers. Our first impulse, when confronted with a problem or obstacle of some sort, is to act—either to take charge ourselves or to light a fire under someone else. We respond in this way because we believe that doing something can make a difference—that individuals, you and I, can actively influence events. We are an activist culture. Our experience as a nation has been to face and overcome serious obstacles, whence our strong faith in the power of doing.

Our Russian friend Natasha lives in a different universe; she believes that the individual is limited in what he or she can do, that many obstacles are truly insurmountable, and there is, therefore, no point in getting excited—in *doing* something—when elevators break down (or roads are impassable or the cow dies). When such a person confronts a broken elevator, her first impulse may very well be to do nothing, to just wait and see what happens next. This resignation or fatalism, which should not be confused with passivity, probably derives in part from the physical hardships of life in Russia; there wasn't much you could *do* about the wind from the steppes or acute shortages of vegetables. Your goal was to endure. And it may also be a legacy of centuries of serfdom, when one (if one was a serf) really did not feel that one had much scope for changing one's life.

This is not to say Natasha doesn't mind that the elevator is broken, isn't inconvenienced by it, or doesn't wish it were fixed, merely that she has no sense that her doing something about it would make the slightest difference. Her immediate instinct is not to act but to cope.

3. Class of '97

To Karen, it's rather straightforward: if you enter college in 1993, you will graduate four years later, in 1997. This is the presumption, unless the unexpected happens. But Americans don't put much stock in the unexpected. Indeed, if the unexpected should happen, chances are we will manipulate the situation to reach our original goal, providing it still matters to us. This is the American norm of self-determination, captured perfectly in the expression "Where there's a will there's a way."

From Carmen's point of view, it is arrogant, if not preposterous, to say with any certainty what is going to happen four years from today. Carmen could die tomorrow, get married next week, or move to Japan next year. Alternatively, the university might burn down, go out of business, or stop offering Carmen's major. Americans start from the presumption that we can control external events and stand up to forces of nature—that come hell or high water, we can achieve our stated goal. But hell and high water count for much more in Carmen's culture, which starts from the presumption that many events are beyond our control. One can go ahead and make plans, of course, but one shouldn't become too fond of or come to depend too much on them. Whenever it wishes, fate can intervene. Americans believe in fate, but on the whole we're not terribly impressed by it.

4. Lucky for Hassan

We would call this cheating; Abdullah calls it helping a friend. For one thing, he may not want Hassan to be embarrassed by doing poorly on the test. Avoiding shame—especially public embarrassment—is a paramount Arab value. For another, Abdullah wants to be cooperative: in this case, he will help Hassan; in another case, perhaps Hassan will help him. In that way, the two of them face life's challenges together and fare rather better than each might on his own. What purpose is to be served by Abdullah keeping what he knows to himself when he could help someone else by sharing it?

For her part, Ms. Anderson no doubt sees this test as a chance to find out what Hassan and Abdullah know. If Hassan doesn't know very much about the subject, this test will motivate him to go back and learn, which will only be to his benefit in the future; that is, at some point down the road Hassan may need this information, and if he doesn't know it, to whom is he going to turn?

Notice the assumption here (one which Hassan would not understand): that in the end each of us ultimately has only our own self to rely on. Self-reliance may be a key American value, but the Arab view would be that you would always have your primary group (family or intimate friends) to turn to if you needed help, just as family and friends can always depend on you if *they* need help. The American saying, "To stand on your own two feet" doesn't resonate in many cultures.

5. Hannah from Bavaria

A nice break for Otto: he won't have to speak English all night. What David is assuming is that two people from the same country, especially if they are outside their country, would have enough in common to enjoy and be comfortable chatting with one another. But Germans are not us; even if Otto lived next door to

Hannah in Bavaria, they wouldn't necessarily know each other because they could very well be from entirely different backgrounds and social classes—which is precisely the case, and there are several clues to that effect in the dialogue. The first thing Otto does is to ask what the woman's name is, for her last name may very well tell him immediately whether he has anything in common with her. Indeed, depending on that name, Otto may have more in common with David or any of his American guests than with Hannah. Alas, David is not very helpful; he gives Hannah's first name, but not her last, which would probably tell Otto her social class or at least what region of the country she's from.

But that information is not far behind, for we learn that Hannah lives on a small farm in Bavaria. Otto, or Mr. von Klein if you prefer, is a diplomat, probably an ambassador (his wife is hosting a reception at the embassy). There wouldn't be many Bavarian farmers in his social circle. He and Hannah won't have much to talk about (and won't be very comfortable doing it). Indeed, it will probably be the first time in their lives that either has talked to someone like the other.

Again, the American presumption here is one of inherent equality or what we might call "alikeness," that underneath all our various superficial differences, people are pretty much the same. In many cultures, the presumption is that underneath our various superficial differences, we are all deeply different.

6. Helping Miss Thomas

Miss Thomas comes from what has been called a monochronic culture (as opposed to the polychronic world of Roberto). Among the prominent features of such a culture are lines at the post office, precise schedules, and one-on-one conversations. In a monochronic culture, you get the exclusive attention of whomever you're talking to, and your business is completed before the business of someone else is started. (Note, in passing, how small children in a monochronic culture deviate from this norm and are always interrupting Mommy or Daddy, which is to say talking to Mommy when she is talking to Daddy.)

Polychronic cultures are less linear and more dynamic; several transactions are carried out at the same time. It's rude for Roberto, for example, to ignore Octavio—who has, after all, walked into the store—just because he hasn't finished Miss Thomas's business yet. (Miss Thomas, were she a Latina, would find Roberto's ignoring of Octavio very unusual and feel quite uncomfortable.) It's not so much that Roberto has stopped helping Miss Thomas, but that he has now started helping Octavio and Rosita. If you are meeting with someone in a polychronic culture, don't expect him or her to close the door and have all calls held.

7. No More Pills

Mr. Brown's on a mission here: to find the medicine that will bring an end to Mr. Patel's pain. There can be no question but that there is such a medicine, for as we all know pain and suffering are not natural. They are abnormal and can be contained and controlled, if not eliminated altogether. If this medicine doesn't work, then that one will; if this doctor can't fix me, then another one can.

Which is not exactly Mr. Patel's position. While he may try this medicine and that, he will eventually reach a point where he concludes that this particular pain must simply be endured, that like pleasure and happiness, pain and suffering are part of life and must run their natural course. They come; they manifest themselves; and they pass.

Most Americans, who aren't very impressed by the external world, tend to regard themselves as the masters of their fate. Sure, fate sends things our way, but we don't have to accept them. There's no excuse, save laziness, for being beaten. If you're sick, it's your own fault, though death, admittedly, still poses a problem; it's the one stroke of fate we haven't yet figured out how to cope with, which is probably part of the reason many Americans hate to talk about death. In her book *Brit-Think, Ameri-Think*, the veteran America watcher, Jane Walmsley, notes that "the single most important thing to know about Americans— the attitude which *truly* distinguishes them from the British, and explains much superficially odd behavior—is that *Americans think that death is optional.*"[1]

8. Freelancing

Most American editors would be likely to evaluate potential contributors on the merit of their writing. And they wouldn't need or necessarily want anyone to speak for that work or for that person (and might even find it suspect.) Either the writing is good (and the person gets the assignment) or it isn't (and he or she doesn't). In England, where Jeremy lives, the work would be important too, perhaps even the deciding factor, but it also matters what kind of person Jeremy is. Is he—as the British really do say—the right sort? And that means more than is he a competent writer.

This is why Jeremy can't just send off his clips and leave it at that. The clips speak for his abilities, but someone has to speak for the man. This is also why he says to Marge, "Any help you could give me would be most appreciated." What he wants is a cover letter from Marge or a phone call to someone Marge knows in the business, some kind of personal connection which will by its very nature serve to vouch for Jeremy in a way that his writing alone cannot.

Again, this is the notion of judging people by their achievements, in this case, the quality of their work. In a culture where one *is* largely what one *does*, the work speaks for the person. There is no need for any other measure, for an independent assessment of the person; the work and the person behind it are one and the same.

9. Dinner on Wednesday

Mr. Ozawa, a friend of Mr. Sogo and Mr. Collins, has become president of the company, which is to say, among other things, that he now occupies a higher rank than his old friend Sogosan. For this reason, it would be presumptuous of Mr. Sogo to accept Collins's invitation to dinner, for if Sogo accepts, he is in effect declaring that he is on the same level as Mr. Ozawa. It is now Sogo's lot in life to defer to Mr. Ozawa and respect their differences in rank.

As soon as Collins heard about the promotion, he should have known it would be impossible for Sogo to accept the dinner invitation and, indeed, that under these new circumstances it was inappropriate even to make it. This, of course, is precisely why Sogo mentioned the promotion in the first place. Notice that when Collins still doesn't make the connection, Sogo signals him again that he won't be coming: "I'll pass on your invitation. I'm sure Ozawa-san will be very pleased to see you."

There is, incidentally, still a chance that Mr. Sogo may come. When Sogo passes on the invitation to his boss, Mr. Ozawa, it's possible Ozawa will invite him to come along (as Mr. Sogo and Mr. Collins are, after all, old friends). And if Mr. Ozawa does the inviting, superior to subordinate, it is quite appropriate for Sogo to accept (after offering the obligatory refusals and protestations about being in the way, etc.).

10. Neighbors

In a classless society, such as the United States strives to be, where we're all theoretically equals, proximity is quite naturally a factor in whom we know and associate with. While living next to someone won't inevitably lead to friendship or a deeper relationship, there's no reason why it should not. In any case it will almost always lead to a casual acquaintanceship. It's expected one will be friendly to everyone, and certainly to people one sees every day.

This doesn't apply in much of the world, especially not here in the case of Helga and her neighbor. If there is no other basis for a relationship, such as similar social or class backgrounds, then proximity alone doesn't qualify. Nor is there any sense of having to be friendly to people one does not know; polite, yes, but friendly, no.

Americans are almost predisposed to be open. Europeans, on the other hand, are predisposed to be closed. "Europeans try to not need new people," Stuart Miller observes in his book, *Understanding Europeans,* and then goes on to quote anthropologist Edward Hall's well-known observation that in many cultures proximity "means nothing. The fact that you live next door to a family does not entitle you to visit, borrow from or socialize with them or your children to play with theirs."[2] The Japanese have a similar view. When you see a stranger, one proverb says, suspect him of being a thief.

11.   Near the Family

A cultural assumption shared by many Americans is that dependence, if not bad, is at least suspect. Parents raise their children to be independent, to stand on their own two feet. Somewhere deep in our psyche there lurks the conviction that in the end we have only ourselves to fall back on.

So Cathy assumes that Vincenzo, an Italian about to graduate from the university, is ready and even eager to strike out on his own, that the time has come to establish his independence and self-reliance, and that he will live somewhere near his parents. But of course Vincenzo isn't going to live near his parents; he's going to live *with* them—and be quite content doing so. It would be unthinkable in his circumstances to be working down the street—or on the other side of town, for that matter—and not live at home. In his culture, parents raise their children to be dependent on the family, not in the sense of being helpless but in the sense of relying on the family for advice and support and regarding the family, rather than one's self, as the primary focus in life. Italians, by the way, identify readily with the rallying cry of the Three Musketeers, "One for all and all for one." One can't help suspecting that had the hearty trio hailed from Boston or Chicago, their motto would undoubtedly have been "Every man for himself," which wouldn't have worked quite as well.

12.   Something Personal

On the whole, Europeans take longer to make friends. As we noted above, for a number of reasons Europeans are predisposed to be closed. Quoting Stuart Miller again: "The private self will not be exhibited by Europeans....The European... regards openness as obscene. This defensive concealment and

mistrust paradoxically help [him] to develop and sustain relationships. Because he refuses to reveal anything about himself
easily, those to whom he does show himself, even a little, are
apprehended as true familiars."[3]

Alain may have known this person Pierre Gallimart for a
year, but it does not follow at all that they have become intimates. Our friend Deborah has probably seen them together a
lot and jumped to the conclusion that they have, which might
be true of two Americans who have known each other a year
and often lunched together. You *can*, after all, get an American's
life story over lunch at a truck stop, but it would take many
lunches and many stops to accomplish this on the Continent.
This doesn't necessarily mean that American friendships are
more shallow (though they do tend to be opportunistic), but only
that many of our friendships are rather casual; we make—and
end—them rather easily. In many other cultures, especially societies that are less mobile than ours, friendships are a more
serious matter and are usually made for life.

English, interestingly enough, has only one form for the second person: *you* (though we did once have *thou*). Our language
thus does not permit us to distinguish with a pronoun between
casual and deeper relationships. German and French, to name
only two languages, have both familiar and formal forms of *you*
(*du* and *Sie*, *tu* and *vous*), and the decision to use one over the
other is significant. There was a time not so long ago when two
Germans commonly marked the shift from *Sie* to *du*, from being
acquaintances to being intimates, with a formal ceremony, usually a dinner. The Thai language, to put all this in perspective,
has twelve ways to say *you*.

13. We Miss You

Susan has put Yang in a very awkward position for an Asian,
one in which he seemingly cannot avoid being insensitive (in
this case, by causing her to lose face). The dilemma for Yang is
how to answer Susan's question without giving offense. He has
just told her that he likes his new job; so when she asks him if
he's glad he left B&G, he can hardly say no. At the same time, if

he says yes, it would be an implicit slight against Susan who, after all, still works there. Yang's only recourse, which he seizes immediately, is to change the subject.

While it is true, incidentally, that Susan would probably not take it personally if Yang said he was glad to be away from B&G, an Asian would not instinctively assume this and would, in any case, want to err on the side of caution. From his perspective, Yang must think Susan boorish to have put him in this embarrassing position and obliged him to change the subject so clumsily.

Once again we would point out that by American standards, Susan is not being insensitive here; the problem, of course, is that she's not being judged by American standards. We say this to reemphasize that from the point of view of most Americans, the people we are meeting in these pages are in fact quite sensitive, i.e., for the most part, their behavior is very appropriate. It is only when the context changes that that same behavior becomes insensitive. As we noted earlier, insensitivity is really little more than sensitivity out of its element.

14. Fathers and Sons

Lieutenant Aziz is taken aback by the degree of independence Colonel Post's sons will have in deciding what they want to do in life. In a culture which values and encourages independence and self-reliance, this might seem natural. But in Lieutenant Aziz's Arab culture, where the family—not the individual—is the smallest unit of survival, for children to make such an important decision without consulting and, to a large degree, following the advice of the parents would be quite out of the ordinary. Children see themselves first as members of the family unit and only then as individuals in their own right. This is not to say that they do not have a sense of personal identity, only that a strong component of that identity is provided by the role or roles each person plays within the family (e.g., oldest son/ brother, daughter-in-law/wife, youngest son/youngest uncle on the maternal side, etc.). Each of these roles carries its own unique set of characteristics and responsibilities, and these in turn go a long way toward defining the individual.

In such a culture, the notion of a separate self quite outside the family is not well developed. So, of course, individuals from these cultures would want to consult with the family on every important decision, whether the choice of a career or, for that matter, of a spouse. After all, one can always learn to love one's spouse, but if the family doesn't approve, that's another matter. Indeed, even if one doesn't learn to love one's spouse, mutual respect will do, and meanwhile the main requirement—family harmony—will have been satisfactorily achieved. And that matters much more in the grand scheme. (See dialogue 17 for another view of this issue.) In Lieutenant Aziz's culture, the worst thing that can happen is to be alienated from one's family. It is equivalent to being stripped of one's identity, and in a practical sense it could seriously undermine one's physical well-being.

15. Humble Beginnings

The United States is the land of rags to riches (followed, in some cases, by a return to rags). In other words, ours is a meritocracy, not an aristocracy. Anybody can be anything if he or she wants it badly enough and tries hard enough. (Or that's the theory, anyway.) You can be a peanut farmer and still become president of the United States. Indeed, we tend to hold the self-made man or woman in even higher regard than the individual born to wealth and opportunity. If one has humble roots and overcomes them—and the assumption here is that one ought to want to do this—one is likely to point to this achievement with some pride. Or at the very least, not to hide it.

Not so in other places, where although one can perhaps achieve one's way into power and success, the self-made individual is not accorded the same status as someone born into the upper class. One is an *arriviste*, as the French say; one has arrived in the upper class, which is quite different from being born there. And if you should have the good fortune to transcend humble origins, you would have the good sense to keep quiet about it. It's not an achievement, in other words; it's an aberration and, all things being equal, one would not wish to be regarded largely as a quirk of fate.

Ralph's going on about the newness of his wealth and his family's peasantlike origins is not likely to impress Henri, who is probing to find out just this sort of information. With such a background, Henri must be thinking, the next generation of Ralphs might easily disappear back into the obscurity whence they came, and there is little reason, therefore, to take this exception to the rule very seriously. If the Ralphs can sustain their good fortune for several generations and plant roots in the aristocracy, then they would be worthy of one's serious attention.

"Class consciousness has always been muted in America," Stuart Miller writes. "But to this day in a great many European countries, when you walk into a cafe, shop or pub, the locals look you over as if they are estimating your place. And when you get into a discussion of politics with a European, he will express astonishment at the kind of people who head our government—a haberdasher, a peanut farmer, an actor—people not suited for the top."[4]

16. Depression

As a rule, Americans try very hard to be happy. Indeed, we regard happiness not merely as a boon we enjoy from time to time—something pleasant that life doles out on occasion—but as a virtual imperative. If one is down, one feels almost obliged to do something about it, for it is the prevailing belief that unhappiness is both unnatural and abnormal. The norm, in other words, is to be happy. If one's friend is down, then of course one wants to do all one can to help—to bring the person back to normal. So it is that Charles is quite naturally roused to action by the news that Anatoly is depressed.

For her part, Tatyana's confusion stems from her very Russian belief that happiness is no more the norm than sadness or depression, that each is a natural and inevitable part of life, and that one is just as likely to occur as the other. Given this acceptance of the normality of sadness, she sees no reason to *do* anything about Anatoly's depression, to fix it, as it were, for there's really nothing broken.

Why this American insistence on being happy? It probably

relates to our belief in the power of individuals to shape events and control their own destinies. If we really are masters of our fate and captains of our souls, as the poet wrote, then there's no excuse for being unhappy. If one is upset by a given set of circumstances, one simply does something to change them. (Note how happiness, or at least the pursuit thereof, is actually enshrined in our Declaration of Independence as one of mankind's "inalienable rights.")

This isn't to say Russians wouldn't prefer to be happy or enjoy being sad, but only that they aren't unhinged by depression. You can only be thrown by depression if you believe happiness is ultimately a matter of choice.

17. Wedding Bells

For the reasons sketched in dialogue 14 above, the more traditional people in some cultures sometimes enter arranged marriages. Fatima's son will meet his bride-to-be in good time, though he probably has a pretty good idea whom his family is going to pick out for him—if not the precise girl, then at least the most likely families under consideration. After all, they're not going to marry him to a family they don't know very well. What's important here is that considerations of social standing, wealth, and family honor are all satisfied. If these major elements are in place, the union is almost certain to be satisfactory to all the parties involved, which includes the bride and groom of course, but extends well beyond them.

For their part, the bride and groom aren't going to reject lightly the partners so carefully and painstakingly chosen for them. The honor of the two familes is at stake for one thing, and, for another, the two young people would not hastily risk their own emotional and even physical well-being by breaking with their families and being alienated therefrom. As Margaret Nydell has written in her book, *Understanding Arabs:* "A Westernized Arab once equated the feelings of an Arab father whose son refuses to accept the family's choice of a bride with the feelings of a Western father who discovers that his son is on drugs."[5]

Endnotes

1. Jane Walmsley, *Brit-Think, Ameri-Think* (New York: Penguin Books, 1987), 2.

2. Stuart Miller, *Understanding Europeans* (Santa Fe: John Muir Publications, 1987), 44.

3. Ibid., 43, 47.

4. Ibid., 72.

5. Margaret Nydell, *Understanding Arabs* (Yarmouth, ME: Intercultural Press, 1987), 5-6.

3

The Workplace: Dialogues 18-49

It's impossible to guess what responses to a given set of
circumstances or surroundings may be going through
the head of someone from the other side of the world.

Philip Glazebrook
Journey to Kars

Dialogues, as we've said, can occur anywhere. The exchanges
in this chapter take place on the job, and although you may
recognize some themes from the social sphere, there are a number of new issues here that are more common to the world of
work: the proper relationship between superiors and subordinates, for example, or issues such as problem solving, giving feed-
back, the role of the supervisor, delegating responsibility, decision making, motivating employees, and the attitude toward hierarchy and the chain of command.

Needless to say, people don't leave their culture at home

when they go to work. Culture is in the person, not the setting
or the context (though different dimensions of culture are manifest in different settings). In the modern world, workplaces are
coming to look increasingly alike, but we shouldn't be fooled by
surface similarities. A computer station may look much the same
around the globe, but the operators sitting at those stations are
as different in their values and attitudes as their computers are
similar.

Nor is it necessary anymore to go abroad to be in a culturally diverse workplace. If you supervise or work alongside or
under someone from another culture, then you are probably
inflicting dialogues on others on a regular basis. Just ask the
American nurse supervised by the Indian-born neurosurgeon
or the manager of any McDonald's or big-city hotel. In this
regard, you can either picture the dialogues in this chapter as
taking place overseas or just down the street.

18. Falling Behind

COL. GARCIA: Yes, we know that, Colonel Wilson.

COL. WILSON: This battalion has not been doing as
much as it could.

COL. GARCIA: Yes, yes.

COL. WILSON: I've told Sergeant Diaz that if we
don't get a few projects started
before the end of the year, we'll be
falling behind some of the other
units.

COL. GARCIA: Yes, some units have fewer projects.

19. Options

MS. CARROLL: There are several ways we can do
this.

MRS. RAFIK: Yes. I'm sure.

MS. CARROLL: If we seek donations, we'll probably
get them. But that will take time.

MRS. RAFIK: Yes. You're right.

MS. CARROLL: If we spend our own money, we can start right away, but we'll have to go in debt.

MRS. RAFIK: Most probably.

MS. CARROLL: Or we could ask for an advance on our fourth-quarter profits.

MRS. RAFIK: That's possible too.

MS. CARROLL: So what do you think?

MRS RAFIK: I think we should pick and get started.

MS. CARROLL: But we have to decide first.

MRS. RAFIK: Of course.

20. Waiting for the Contract

MS. WARREN: Is the contract ready then?

MR. CHAO: I'm afraid not. Mr. Sung still hasn't prepared it.

MS. WARREN: He's not very efficient, is he?

MR. CHAO: Not anymore. But he used to be an excellent worker. I've been trying to find out what's wrong.

MS. WARREN: What did he say to you?

21. A Possible Candidate

MS. MILLER: Have you finished writing that job advertisement yet?

MRS. DeJESUS: Not quite.

MS. MILLER: Don't take too long. Filling that vacancy is a priority.

MRS. DeJESUS: I agree. Actually, I think I know of a possible candidate.

MS. MILLER: You do? Who?

MRS. DeJESUS: He's my youngest nephew, Eduardo. A good boy.

MS. MILLER: Great! Tell him to apply.

22. More Study

MR. JOHNSON: What did you think of the new plan?

MR. TRUDEAU: Seems OK, but I'm still studying it. I want to be sure.

MR. JOHNSON: Still studying it after three weeks? It's not that complicated.

MR. TRUDEAU: There are one or two aspects that might be a problem.

MR. JOHNSON: Oh, I know that. But we should put it in place and work the bugs out later.

MR. TRUDEAU: Seriously?

23. A Pat on the Back

MR. KANEDA: Are you satisfied then, Ms. Walden, with the work of the accounting division?

MS. WALDEN: Very much. Their output has improved tremendously.

MR. KANEDA: They're very proud of their work.

MS. WALDEN: As soon as you put Mr. Yamamoto in charge, things began to turn around.

MR. KANEDA: Yes, the whole team is working very smoothly now.

MS. WALDEN: Will you be giving Mr. Yamamoto some kind of recognition then?

MR. KANEDA: Excuse me?

MS. WALDEN: You know. An award or something?

MR. KANEDA: I hardly think so. We wouldn't want to embarrass him after all he has done.

24. Rough Edges

MR. PIERCE: Enrique, I'd like you to work with Paul on this project.

ENRIQUE: Yes, sir.

MR. PIERCE: You're hesitating. Is something wrong?

ENRIQUE: Excuse me, sir, but I don't work very well with Paul. It's my fault, I'm sure.

MR. PIERCE: No it isn't. I know about Paul. But don't let him get to you. Sure, he's a little rough around the edges, but he really knows programming. And that's what counts.

ENRIQUE: Yes, sir.

25. The Flu

SARAH: I was hoping we could have that meeting of the sales team tomorrow morning.

FELICE: Actually, my daughter has some kind of flu and I was going to take her to the doctor tomorrow morning.

SARAH: I see. Well, let me check with Bob and see if he can sit in for you. Shouldn't be any problem. I'll let you know.

FELICE: Thank you.

SARAH: Don't mention it.

26. A New Boss

MS. SPENCER: Ah, Victoria. Please sit down.

VICTORIA: Thank you, ma'am.

MS. SPENCER: I wanted to ask you if everything's going OK with your job?

VICTORIA: Yes. Very much so, ma'am.

MS. SPENCER: It's just that ever since I took over here people have been coming to me with questions I know you can answer. Better than I, in fact, as I'm new to the London office and you've been working for us here for ten years.

VICTORIA: Yes.

MS. SPENCER: Maybe if they asked you first, it would save some time.

VICTORIA: But they do ask me first.

27. Tea

MR. WALKER: I was wondering, Mr. Singh, if the books I'd ordered had come yet?

MR. SINGH: Yes, yes. The books have arrived at the storehouse.

MR. WALKER: Oh, good. Maybe I can pick them up on my way home from school.

MR. SINGH: No, no. I will send someone to bring them for you.

MR. WALKER: That's very kind, but I don't mind going along. In case they need help.

MR. SINGH: No, no. You wait here, Mr. Walker. And we will drink tea.

28. *Dedication*

MS. LEWIS: As you know, we've had many complaints about Mr. Barzini.

MRS. FERMI: What kind of complaints?

MS. LEWIS: He's very slow in his work and some of our people aren't getting paid promptly.

MRS. FERMI: Yes. Mr. Barzini's been with us a great many years; he's not as efficient as he used to be. His age is beginning to catch up with him.

MS. LEWIS: So you agree?

MRS. FERMI: Definitely. After so many years of dedicated service, we can't expect him to perform as he used to. We'll be hiring someone new.

MS. LEWIS: That's good to know. But I feel bad for Mr. Barzini. How's he taking it?

MRS. FERMI: Taking it?

MS. LEWIS: Losing his job, I mean.

MRS. FERMI: Oh, he's not losing his job.

29. *The Thinker*

RICHARD: Did Claude turn in his final draft yet?

ISABELLE: No, he's still working on it. You know Claude, always thinking and pondering.

RICHARD: But I needed that report last week.

ISABELLE: I know. Claude never meets his deadlines; it's a real problem. But his ideas are so wonderful, aren't they?

RICHARD: I've complained about him twice to Monsieur Cardin, but he doesn't do anything.

ISABELLE: You've complained. Why?

30. An Opportunity in Monterey

MR. MARTIN: Hector. Come in and sit down.

HECTOR: Thank you, Mr. Martin.

MR. MARTIN: I've got a little proposition for you. A friend of mine up in our Monterey branch needs a production supervisor. He asked me if I knew of anyone who might be interested.

HECTOR: I can ask. We don't have any relations up in Monterey, but I know a few people.

MR. MARTIN: I was thinking of you.

HECTOR: Me?

MR. MARTIN: Yes. It would be a nice promotion for you. We'd miss you down here, but we wouldn't want to stand in your way.

HECTOR: In my way? Are you not satisfied with my work?

MR. MARTIN: Are you kidding? I wouldn't recommend you if I didn't think you were the best.

31. The Overdue Claim

MS. HARRIS: I was wondering if my claim has been processed yet.

MISS CHEN: No, not just yet.

MS. HARRIS: How long does it take?

MISS CHEN: No longer than two weeks.

MS. HARRIS: But it's been four weeks.

MISS CHEN: This is unusual.

MS. HARRIS: Maybe it's lost.

MISS CHEN: Oh no. It can't be lost.

32. Performance Evaluation

MR. COYLE: Thanks for coming, Khalil. Let's go over this evaluation together, shall we?

KHALIL: Whatever you'd like, sir.

MR. COYLE: As you know, you're quite strong in most areas. There are just a couple of areas where you could be stronger.

KHALIL: I see.

MR. COYLE: One is in writing, which isn't easy for you, is it?

KHALIL: No, sir.

MR. COYLE: And the other is in identifying training needs. Some of your staff could use more computer training in particular.

KHALIL: Yes.

MR. COYLE: Anyway, it's all written here. You can read it. Otherwise, no serious problems.

KHALIL: I'm very sorry to disappoint you, sir.

33. A Question for Miss Yoshikawa

THERESA: That was an excellent presentation. You and Dr. Nagai must have worked very hard on this.

MISS YOSHIKAWA: I was very honored to be asked by Dr. Nagai to assist him on this project. He's my thesis advisor, you know.

THERESA: Well, you were very good. He's lucky to have found you. I had a question about a point you made at the end.

MISS YOSHIKAWA: Yes, of course. Let me just get Dr. Nagai.

THERESA: Oh, don't bother him; he's talking to some other people. Anyway, it's about a point that you made.

MISS YOSHIKAWA: I see. Can I get you some tea?

34. A Helping Hand

CARL: Hey, Juan. Is everything OK?

JUAN: Yes, sir. I was just explaining to Raul here about the new drill press. Some of the men aren't sure about it yet.

CARL: I know. Actually, I overheard you; what you were telling Raul isn't exactly right.

JUAN: No?

CARL: No. You have to turn on the fan *before* you switch on the water jet, not after. Now try it, Raul. [Pause.] Yes. That's it. Any more problems with this, Juan, just come and ask me. That's what I'm here for.

JUAN: Thank you, sir.

35. Calling in Sick

MS. PARKER: Sit down, Miss Lim. I'm worried about you. I've noticed you've been calling in sick a lot the last month.

MISS LIM: I'm sorry, ma'am.

MS. PARKER: Ever since I promoted you to office manager. Is the job too much for you?

MISS LIM: Perhaps, ma'am.

MS. PARKER: I don't know what to do. I would have given the job to Mr. Sen or Miss Jiu, but they're not nearly as efficient. Especially these last few weeks.

MISS LIM: Oh no, ma'am. They are very good, and they have been here much longer than I.

36. Choices

ARABELLA: I liked the man from Liverpool.

BOB: David Symes? Why is that?

ARABELLA: I liked his style and his manners. He makes a very good first impression. He's also very well spoken.

BOB: I guess you're right. But I wonder about his technical background. The man from Oxford seemed a bit stronger.

ARABELLA: The one with the loud tie? Yes, he was stronger.

37. Moving Up

GEORGE: You must be very proud of your sales team, Gaston.

GASTON: I am, very. They've done an excellent job.

GEORGE: Makes you look pretty good, too.

GASTON: Yes, probably so.

GEORGE: Maybe the top man will notice. I hear the position of vice president for marketing is vacant.

GASTON: Yes. They're looking for a replacement. We hope they find someone soon.

GEORGE: Maybe this is your chance.

GASTON: My chance?

GEORGE: To make your move.

GASTON: My move?

GEORGE: To move up.

GASTON: To v.p. for marketing? Me? I doubt it. What a disaster that would be!

38. Explanations

MS. WRIGHT: Miss. Chung. What can I do for you?

MISS CHUNG: Excuse me. I need some help with this new machine.

MS. WRIGHT: Of course. Let me explain it again.

MISS CHUNG: I asked Li, but she couldn't help me.

MS. WRIGHT: No, she hasn't tried it yet.

MISS CHUNG: It's a little bit complicated.

MS. WRIGHT: It's very complicated, but after I explained it to you and asked you if you understood, you said yes.

MISS CHUNG: Yes. Please excuse me.

39. A Software Upgrade

BRENDA: I've heard there's a new version of that software program we use in our accounting system.

ANDREI: The program we have works quite well.

BRENDA: I know, but this new one's bound to be better. I think I'll order it and look it over.

ANDREI: We're all quite used to this program.

BRENDA: It can't hurt to check the new one out.

ANDREI: Why do you say that?

40. Writing a Report

MS. COLSON: How is the evaluation going, Ram?

RAM: It's finished, ma'am. We can start on the report anytime now.

MS. COLSON: Good. How long do you think it will take?

RAM: Ma'am?

MS. COLSON: To write the report.

RAM: I couldn't say, ma'am.

MS. COLSON: You don't know how long it will take?

RAM: When would you like it, ma'am?

MS. COLSON: Well, I want to give you enough time to do a good job.

RAM: We'll do a good job, ma'am.

41. A Nuisance

BILL: How did it go with Nigel?

MARY: Much better than I expected. These English are hard to figure.

BILL: What happened? Did you explain everything to him?

MARY: Yes, completely. I said we were very sorry but we simply weren't going to be able to meet the deadline.

BILL: And?

MARY: He just said, "That's a bit of a nuisance" and changed the subject.

BILL: That's great!

42.　Saturday Shift

MR. JONES:　It looks like we're going to have to keep the production line running on Saturday.

MR. WU:　I see.

MR. JONES:　Can you come in on Saturday?

MR. WU:　Yes. I think so.

MR. JONES:　That'll be a great help.

MR. WU:　Yes. Saturday's a special day, did you know?

MR. JONES:　How do you mean?

MR. WU:　It's my son's birthday.

MR. JONES:　How nice. I hope you all enjoy it very much.

MR. WU:　Thank you. I appreciate your understanding.

43.　Dr. de Leon

MS. PORTER:　I heard the board has chosen a new CEO.

MR. DOMINGO:　Yes, they've appointed Dr. Manuel Cabeza de Leon of the de Leon family.

MS. PORTER:　Who is he?

MR. DOMINGO:　It's an old family with large land-holdings in Guadalajara Province.

MS. PORTER:　But what's his background?

MR. DOMINGO:　I just told you.

MS. PORTER:　I mean does he know anything about the textile industry.

MR. DOMINGO:　I don't know.

MS. PORTER:　Do you think he's a good choice?

MR. DOMINGO:　Dr. de Leon? I'm sure.

44. Two New Nursing Stations

MR. KHOURI: Would you like to see the two new nursing stations?

MR. COMPTON: Stations? I thought we agreed to build one station and, if there was any money left over, to buy some equipment for it so we could start using it.

MR. KHOURI: Yes, but there was enough money to build two stations at once.

MR. COMPTON: But is there any money left over to equip them?

MR. KHOURI: Unfortunately, no.

MR. COMPTON: Then we can't use them!

MR. KHOURI: Not presently. But isn't it good? We used all the money.

45. Thumbs Down

JENNY: How did the meeting go last night?

TOMOKO: It was a very useful discussion.

JENNY: How so?

TOMOKO: We all talked. And Mr. Takeda explained his reservations about the proposal.

JENNY: Did anyone else agree with him?

TOMOKO: No. He was the only one who has some doubts.

JENNY: Then we won the vote.

TOMOKO: Oh, there was no vote, of course. We postponed it.

46. Fourth-Quarter Sales

MS. JOSEPH: Did you see the fourth-quarter sales figures yet?

MR. KARPOV: Yes. Rather bad; down a third from last year.

MS. JOSEPH: We really took a beating.

MR. KARPOV: Yes. We did very poorly.

MS. JOSEPH: Oh, well. We might as well look on the bright side; things can only go up from here.

MR. KARPOV: I'm not so sure. I think the figures could go even lower.

MS. JOSEPH: Well, no point in being gloomy though, is there?

MR. KARPOV: What do you mean?

47. A Call to Personnel

HAROLD: I was wondering if we could hire two temporary people for the next month, to get through this peak period?

RICARDO: I think we'll have to.

HAROLD: I could speak to personnel today.

RICARDO: Did you mention this to Señor Ramos?

HAROLD: The chief? I didn't want to bother him. He's got his hands full with those buyers from Japan. Besides, it's your division. He'll agree to anything you say.

RICARDO: Yes. I'm sure he'll approve.

HAROLD: Good. Then I'll call Miss Garcia in personnel.

48. A New Procedure

MS. COOPER: The new tracking procedure hasn't worked, has it?

MR. WONG: There were some small problems.

MS. COOPER: Whose idea was it anyway?

MR. WONG: We need to learn from this lesson.

MS. COOPER: Yes. It came from Mr. Tung's division, didn't it?

MR. WONG: Many people worked on the proposal.

49. Feasibility Study

MS. WARNER: I thought today we would look at the feasibility of the Ministry's proposed agribusiness project. There are several elements that need to be studied more closely before we can decide whether to commit any funds.

MR. RANJIT: I agree. Perhaps we could begin by discussing who the director of the project will be.

MS. WARNER: That will have to be decided, of course, but first we have to see if the project will fly.

MR. RANJIT: Yes. That's my point.

The Workplace:
Explanatory Notes

18. Falling Behind

Colonel Wilson is trying to light a fire under Colonel Garcia, but he's using the wrong fuel. He's trying to appeal to Colonel Garcia's sense of competition, goading him with the suggestion that if he and his men don't get cracking, their unit is going to fall behind some of the others—in that great race to win.

Colonel Garcia sees things rather differently. If some other units are doing quite well in the area of projects, then his unit need not work so hard. They're all in the same army, after all; why should they compete against each other? For its part, perhaps his unit can distinguish itself in some other regard, in an arena some of the other units might not choose to enter. In any event, competition, at least for its own sake, is certainly not a virtue. On the contrary, an appeal to the spirit of cooperation would probably be more potent in this case.

Competition tends to be better developed in more individu-

alist societies like the United States. In cultures where people
identify more with a primary group than with the self, competition may threaten group harmony, and that, in turn, threatens
the very survival of the group.

19. Options

Ms. Carroll knows there has got to be a right answer here. And
she believes that with enough discussion and careful analysis,
that right answer can be discovered. The way to do this, of course,
is via a methodical and objective examination of all the alterna-
tives, listing their advantages and disadvantages, and then se-
lecting the one that emerges as the best.

Mrs. Rafik isn't so sure. For one thing, she may not believe
that there is one best answer; and for another she may not feel
that even if there is, she and Ms. Carroll can necessarily identify
it. She would rather just select an option, any option, and get
started. If it turns out to be unworkable, then you drop that
option and select another. In the end, will you be any further
behind than if you took weeks to isolate the best option? Moreover, since no one knows what the future holds anyway, any sci-
entific, systematic analysis of the pros and cons of each option
will never be unconditionally valid.

Ultimately this comes down to the differences between a
view of the world as being mechanistic, and therefore predictable, or chaotic, and therefore undependable. If the world is
mechanistic, then it is knowable; that is, its mechanisms or operations can be analyzed, codified, and, to a certain extent,
mastered. But if the world is chaotic and unpredictable, then no
amount of objective analysis is going to reveal the deeper plan
or system that determines its workings. In such a world, one still
does one's best to try to learn and understand—even to plan—
but one proceeds with humility and low expectations.

20. Waiting for the Contract

Ms. Warren instinctively assumes Mr. Chao has gone to Mr.
Sung to find out what's wrong ("What did he say to you?"). While
this might be standard operating procedure in the United States,

for many cultures (one is sorely tempted to say, most) this kind of directness would be highly inappropriate. The problem is the embarrassment or loss of face that both parties would feel: Mr. Sung for being directly confronted with his shortcomings, and Mr. Chao for not knowing enough about the situation to have headed it off in the first place. Indeed, in some cultures, if the boss or supervisor goes directly to the individual involved, this is an indication that the problem is so serious the boss wants the person to resign.

It's not that Mr. Sung's problems should be ignored; it's all in how you find them out. Mr. Chao will ask a third party to approach Mr. Sung and then report back to him. Mr. Sung knows full well that Mr. Chao has instigated the visit and that the intermediary will report back to Mr. Chao, but so long as he is not confronted directly, his dignity and honor remain more or less intact (though it's worth pointing out that he will still need to correct whatever deficiencies he's experiencing).

Americans, who place a high value on directness, do not normally like involving other people in situations like these; it's none of their business. In fact, we call what Mr. Chao is about to do "going behind someone's back." "If you've got a problem," we're likely to say, "then come to me about it." Americans are, in fact, among the most direct of all nationalities; probably only the Israelis, Germans, Australians, and Russians are more direct. Our high regard for straight talk no doubt comes from our love of efficiency on the one hand (straight talk saves time) and our self-reliance on the other (I'm ultimately responsible for my actions so I need to know the unvarnished truth). Beyond that, a culture which places such a high value on getting things done can't afford to beat around the bush.

21. A Possible Candidate

There's a good reason why Mrs. DeJesus hasn't finished writing that job advertisement yet: advertising is a mighty poor way to fill a vacancy. After all, *anyone* can respond to an ad, and what company wants just anyone working for it? What you want is someone you can trust and rely on, someone from the right background, with the right values and the right style and manners.

And it goes without saying that you don't *find* such people, you *know* them. Or someone you know knows them and can therefore vouch for them.

Thus it is that when Mrs. DeJesus mentions her nephew to Ms. Miller, she expects that will solve the matter of the vacancy and make the advertisement unnecessary. Clearly Mrs. DeJesus wouldn't mention her nephew if the young man weren't the right sort of person, and if Eduardo *is* her nephew, then she will know he's the right sort of person. But unaccountably, Ms. Miller tells Mrs. DeJesus to ask Eduardo to *apply* for the job, implying that Eduardo will be subject to some other set of criteria. For Mrs. DeJesus, Eduardo meets the only criterion that really matters.

For Ms. Miller, of course, there is another issue here: is Eduardo the most technically qualified person available? He may be a nice guy, the right sort of person, from a good family, etc., but the bottom line is: can he do the work? This matters to Mrs. DeJesus too—she wouldn't have recommended the boy if he didn't have the necessary basic skills—but Eduardo doesn't have to be a whiz in this regard so long as you can work with him. It's a question of emphasis: for Mrs. DeJesus, the main thing is the boy's personal qualities; whatever skills he needs can always be trained into him. For Ms. Miller, the issue is the skills; the boy's character, though important, is secondary.

In many American organizations the DeJesus approach smacks of favoritism at best and discrimination at worst—and may even be illegal. This is an excellent example of a fundamental cultural norm being written into the law of the land (*your* land, that is). That's fine, you say, but if my company or employer has this regulation and it conflicts with a local cultural norm, what am I supposed to do? You can't ignore the regulation, of course, but you can try to explain the cultural basis for your company's policy. That is, you should not just leave the impression that this is an arbitrary regulation based on expediency but rather take pains to point out that it derives from a cultural notion of what is right and wrong. Your listeners may not agree with your conclusion, but at least they will see you are trying to be reasonable.

22. More Study

Americans take risks—and let the chips fall where they may. The French would rather know where the chips are going to fall, how many, and what size. The Europeans who settled this country—making a dangerous ocean voyage into a completely unknown future—could handle uncertainty, and a streak of that devil-may-care attitude has survived intact in the American character. We like to experiment, to try something new, not because we are dissatisfied with what we have but because we value the new for its own sake. Newer, we feel, is better or at least potentially better. Remember the new Coke? It's not as though the old Coke wasn't selling briskly enough.

Many cultures are skeptical of the new; they presume it to be worse until it is proven to be otherwise. At the very least, the new certainly has no value in and of itself; it may turn out to be good, but the odds are against it. The French have been around a long time; there's very little new under the *soleil*. And what there is, is suspect. Thus, Trudeau is temperamentally inclined to be skeptical about Johnson's new plan; the presumption must be that it's full of snags and difficulties, all of which need to be identified and ironed out ahead of time. When all the risk is thus squeezed out of the plan, then it might be time to very cautiously initiate it (on a pilot basis). So long as there are doubts and uncertainties—so long as there are risks—the plan must be considered unacceptable. There is nothing to be gained from falling on our faces. Trial and error is not the preferred way to do business.

Americans believe if you fall on your face, you get up. Europeans feel that if you fall on your face, no one ever forgets the sight of you sprawled in the mud.

23. A Pat on the Back

Notice how Ms. Walden zeroes in on Mr. Yamamoto, whereas Mr. Kaneda keeps talking about the team and the group. In Japan, one identifies very strongly with one's group; it is the group which achieves and the group which should be recognized (or it is the group which fails and is collectively held responsible). Individuals think of themselves primarily in terms of their group and very much want to be seen as such, cooperating and working in harmony with the other members of the team for the good of all. When there's a choice to be made, the needs or wishes of the individual are usually subordinated to those of the group (which, of course, looks after its individual members in return).

Mr. Yamamoto would be mortified if he were singled out for some kind of recognition. He would not regard what he has done as a personal achievement (which it probably isn't) and would be very much worried about how the members of his team would feel about being overlooked. The solution, of course, is to give the whole division the recognition, being extremely careful not to leave anyone out.

This is not to say, incidentally, that there is no spirit of competition in Japan; there is a great deal of often fierce competition—between groups. Nor is it safe to conclude that individual Japanese never stand out from the group or don't have distinct personalities (including personal strengths and weaknesses), or that Japanese workers are a faceless mass busily churning out Hondas and Walkmans in cheerful and highly coveted obscurity. Individualism may not be the cultural rudder it is in the United States, but individuals—with their myriad idiosyncrasies—most assuredly exist. It's just that the Japanese don't happen to admire, as Americans do, those who stand out from the group.

An American manufacturing company gave its employee-of-the-year award at an annual banquet. In his first year at the plant, a Japanese man won the award and shyly received the plaque. The next year he won it again—and convinced management to give him the plaque in private.

24. Rough Edges

As it turns out, what really counts differs from culture to culture. Knowing your stuff is important in Enrique's Latin culture too, but it's all a question of emphasis. Paul is clearly not an easy person to work with; his style and manners are evidently quite rough. We can assume that he's rude or blunt or just generally insensitive. Enrique may be willing to overlook a lot, but there's a limit. Past that limit, it doesn't matter how much Paul knows about programming.

There's a limit in the United States too, but we tend to value substance—in this case, experience and technical expertise—more than style (and to make a much greater distinction between the two). We'll put up with a lot if, as Mr. Pierce says, the guy knows his stuff. For Enrique, it's not so easy—or wise—to separate the man from his behavior.

Notice, incidentally, how careful Enrique is about his own manners, trying very hard not to be put in a position where he has to criticize Paul. Somehow one can't imagine Paul exhibiting a similar sensibility (though, of course, that is precisely the standard he is being measured against).

25. The Flu

In all honesty, Sarah might be insensitive even by American standards; by Felice's, she's downright boorish. To a Latin, one's family comes before one's work (and one's boss would, of course, understand this). The least Sarah could have done was to express her concern about Felice's daughter. The next thing she could have done was to postpone the meeting. And beyond that she should have offered to help in any way that she could. Sarah may have thought she was helping by arranging for Felice to miss the meeting, but all she was doing was communicating that the real emergency was the one here at work—not the one at Felice's home.

26. A New Boss

Ms. Spencer tends to be rather more practical than Victoria. She thinks if a person knows a thing, then he/she should dispense that information as required. But Victoria is obeying a different (British) dictum, one that says one should not behave in a way above one's station. Ms. Spencer is her boss, above her in the hierarchy, and must be deferred to. For a subordinate to usurp the perceived prerogative of a superior, at least without being given explicit permission to do so, would not be proper. (Even if permission *were* given, it still might not come easily to a Britisher.) So while it's quite true that Victoria knows the answers to questions and Ms. Spencer doesn't, she is only protecting her boss's reputation and dignity by referring the questioners to her. However, if Ms. Spencer then refers these people back to Victoria, Victoria would be quite within her bounds to answer their questions. Having made the necessary gesture of deference, she is free to use her expertise.

This notion of what's proper doesn't count for that much with many Americans. We don't stand on ceremony, as we are wont to say (which is precisely what Victoria is doing here). We are a pragmatic, even utilitarian people; what's proper is what works (and improper is what doesn't). Behind this attitude lurks that vestigial antipathy toward a rigid class system and the attendant practice (not to mention necessity) of keeping people in their place.

27. Tea

Mr. Walker is not sufficiently status conscious to suit Mr. Singh. Indeed, he is shockingly unconcerned about the image he projects. It is the lot of some people in life to carry books and of others to teach, and if the one sort should suddenly turn into the other, then where would we be? For a teacher to be seen carrying books, a manual task, would not only demean him in the eyes of his students, it would be seen as a slur on the importance of education itself. Nor would his colleagues appreciate it.

Mr. Walker comes from a culture which deemphasizes status and class, where a president might send a very positive message by carrying his own suitcase from his helicopter into the White House (or by buying coffee at McDonald's). We don't like people who think they are above certain tasks, who think they are better than someone else. He puts on airs, we say, or she tries to lord it over me—and these aren't compliments. While we readily acknowledge that some people get ahead and others don't—and we think more highly of the former—we are at the same time careful not to imply that those who succeed are somehow inherently superior to those who don't. We struggle mightily with this because we admire achievement so much, but we still recoil at the notion that anything so random as an accident of birth can make one person better than another.

A Peace Corps teacher in a remote village in a Middle Eastern country took an avid interest in the life of his town. At harvest time, he wanted to join the men as they brought in the wheat crop. On the appointed morning, he went out to the fields with the fathers of his students and stood ready as the headman assigned everyone to his place. Some men were to cut, others to gather, others were in charge of transport. As the headman approached the teacher, the latter asked, "And where is my place?" The headman looked at him for a moment and then answered, "In the classroom."

28. Dedication

Ms. Lewis assumes that if Mr. Barzini is not performing efficiently, then his job must be in jeopardy, which is to say that she assumes output or production is all that really matter in judging a worker's usefulness.

While output no doubt matters to Mrs. Fermi too, clearly something else does as well. The bottom line, as we would say, seems to be a bit broader here in Italy. Among the factors also taken into consideration are loyalty, dedication, and years of experience. These can contribute to the bottom line and maybe even to cost-effectiveness.

On the whole, Americans tend to be uncomfortable with intangibles; we don't trust what we can't quantify. Accordingly, we believe that only objective measures are truly fair, and since we can objectively measure production, then it naturally becomes a reliable standard of performance. But how can we measure dedication or loyalty? And if we can't measure them, then how can we use them to judge our employees?

29. The Thinker

What good are all of Claude's ideas, Richard thinks, if he can't meet deadlines? With such a keen mind and such wonderful ideas, Isabelle wonders, why should someone like Claude have to worry about turning reports in on time? In the end, your view of Claude comes down to how you feel about ideas.

As it happens, the French (and many Europeans) have a deep respect for ideas and, as a consequence, for intellectuals; the development of the mind and the intellect is a legitimate pursuit. Many French can and do get quite excited about ideas, heatedly arguing philosophy, politics, or literature into the wee hours. It's no coincidence that one of the most popular TV shows in France is "Apostrophes," which is about books (or that "My Word," about the English language, is one of the most popular shows on the BBC). As Lynn Payer has written in *Medicine and Culture*: "One must first understand that the French, more than just about any other nationality, value thinking as an activity in itself. Americans value doers, the French value thinkers."[1] Two French people actually can spend a whole evening discussing Marxism.

Ideas don't have quite the same cachet here in America. It's not that we don't respect ideas or realize their value, but on the whole we are more interested in the practical application of ideas than in ideas for their own sake. We tend to prefer the person who acts to the one who thinks. This strong preference for doing—as opposed to thinking and reflecting—is also the source of that common American practice of putting down talk, as in the expressions: "Talk is cheap," "Actions speak louder than words," and "He's all talk (and no action)." This is all of a piece with the notion that in the end it is what you do—not what you say or think—that really matters.

This is not to say, by the way, that the French don't care about concrete results; it's just that they allow thinkers more latitude.

30. An Opportunity in Monterey

Mr. Martin assumes that if Hector is at all normal, he will be interested in getting ahead in life, which—as we all know—really means getting ahead in his work. In such a world, a promotion is one of the best things life can offer, and Mr. Martin has thoughtfully just dropped one in Hector's lap.

Hector might be interested under the right conditions, but certainly the lure of a promotion, in and of itself, is not sufficient reason to move to Monterey. As he points out, he hasn't got any family in Monterey. To uproot his own family and move to where they have no relatives, merely to get ahead in one's work, is not appealing. Indeed, the notion is so foreign to Hector that he now begins to suspect that Mr. Martin, who can't possibly expect Hector to take this offer seriously, must be trying to tell him something. All Hector can think of is that Mr. Martin is not pleased with his work and wants to get rid of him. Indeed, he may even be asking Hector to quit and has only mentioned the move to Monterey as a gesture to save Hector's face.

The cultural value here is once again the American preoccupation with work and the centrality of work to one's happiness and overall sense of self. It's not so much that Americans don't care about friends and family, about quality of life, but that they see quality of life as inextricably linked to satisfaction and opportunity on the job. Because we identify with doing (as distinguished from being) or, rather, because we see *being* as a function and result of *doing*, anything associated with one's work (especially promotions or, conversely, firings) automatically has repercussions which extend well beyond the workplace, to the very heart of one's self-worth.

31. The Overdue Claim

The issue here is what is known as "face"—and the need to save it. Face means the image one presents to the world, including one's reputation, and naturally one wants one's image or reputation to be as positive as possible. Face is therefore closely linked to the notion of self-esteem or self-worth, and if at all possible one does not want to lose one's face, especially not in public. Left alone, one can pretty well look after one's own face, so the issue is usually the need to be careful to preserve the face of others.

In this example, a potentially embarrassing (or face-losing) thing has happened: someone has evidently lost a claim form. Ms. Harris, not schooled in the matter of face, is just trying to find out what happened to her form, all the while causing Miss Chen increasingly exquisite agonies of humiliation. Because she doesn't understand, Ms. Harris misses all three of Miss Chen's hints that this matter is most embarrassing and should be dropped. The first hint is when Miss Chen says, "No, not just yet." For Miss Chen to have to disappoint a customer like this, to have to admit that a certain service has not been rendered, is humiliating. So much so, in fact, that Miss Chen now fully expects the inquiry will stop before any more damage is done.

But it doesn't. Not picking up on the embarrassment she has caused, Ms. Harris now asks how long it normally takes to process a claim. And Miss Chen, forced to go on, says "No longer than two weeks," signaling to Ms. Harris a second time that something has gone wrong (Miss Chen knows full well how much time has passed here) and Ms. Harris should back off. But she again misses the hint and takes aim anew: "But it's been four weeks."

Miss Chen, very red in the face by now (perhaps even laughing to cover her embarrassment), abandons subtlety and admits that something is wrong—"This is unusual"—convinced that surely now the interrogation will end.

Still it doesn't. Ms. Harris now exceeds all bounds and suggests that the claim is lost. Miss Chen, to save her own face and that of the people she works with, can't possibly admit this, of course. And she doesn't: "It can't be lost," she says, capturing the essence of face in this perfectly phrased response. She doesn't say it *isn't* lost (which it is), but that it *can't* be lost, for that would mean a loss of face for someone—and such a development would be intolerable.

Can so much really be going on here (the reader may wonder)? In brief, yes. While it's true this dialogue nearly sinks beneath the weight of so much analysis, a lot has transpired in—and most especially between—these eight lines. A short exchange can bear a heavy cultural load; in no time, we can be well beyond the limits of shared expectations and mutual understanding.

The reader should not conclude from this explanation that mistakes are overlooked and no one is ever criticized or reprimanded in Chinese culture. Not at all, but criticism is normally expressed indirectly and rarely in such a way as to cause public shame.

32. Performance Evaluation

In many Middle Eastern societies, honor is a paramount virtue. And shame, or the public loss of face, is accordingly the ultimate humiliation. Criticism, therefore, has to be handled with extreme delicacy—which is to say it is to be avoided wherever possible and where that is not possible it should be expressed with the utmost discretion and indirection. With his extreme sensitivity to this matter, Khalil naturally interprets the most fleeting and highly understated reference to a particular mistake or difficulty as criticism of the first order. Imagine, then, how he would interpret a direct statement of criticism such as that given here by Mr. Coyle!

For his part, Mr. Coyle is in fact rather pleased with Khalil's performance all in all, except for one or two areas where he thinks Khalil could improve. But to Khalil, such a blatant and direct statement of his deficiencies can only mean that Mr. Coyle is very disappointed. We must remember here that Khalil naturally assumes Mr. Coyle is bending over backward to be as sensitive as possible to Khalil's honor. If that is true and this is the best Mr. Coyle can do—if this represents absolutely the best face Mr. Coyle can put on the matter—then Khalil's performance must be very poor indeed.

How, then, should Mr. Coyle have handled the matter? Mr. Coyle's proportions are off; he should have spent most of the interview lavishing exaggerated praise on Khalil and then mentioned any shortcomings very briefly in passing at the end. Even then Khalil would have taken the "criticism" seriously, but, his honor having been preserved, he could have withstood the onslaught. One is reminded of the story of the princess and the pea; even through all those mattresses, she could still feel the rub of the little green offender. In his interview, Mr. Coyle left out all the mattresses.

33. A Question for Miss Yoshikawa

Miss Yoshikawa has indeed done a good job and is no doubt quite capable of answering Theresa's question. But that's hardly the point; she is an assistant here, a helper, apparently a graduate student. It would be presumptuous of her to answer Theresa's question so long as Dr. Nagai is still in the room, for that would suggest that she knows as much as Dr. Nagai—which may be quite true, of course; but to act in such a way would be very disrespectful to one's elder and superior.

This is why Miss. Yoshikawa tries to break away from Theresa and get Dr. Nagai and why, when that doesn't work, she then tries to play for time by offering to bring tea. Come what may, she's not going to let Theresa put her in the position of humiliating her professor.

From Theresa's point of view, she simply wants an answer to her question and is going about it in the most efficient way possible: to ask the person who happens to be available at the moment. She means no disrespect and may in fact only be trying to be sensitive by going to Miss Yoshikawa, someone lower down the pecking order, and not bothering the exalted professor with her question.

34. A Helping Hand

Juan is not pleased. To be corrected in public is bad enough, but to be corrected in front of a subordinate—someone he supervises and would be expected to know more than—is especially humiliating. What Carl should have done, of course, is to have taken Juan aside later and, without even mentioning the "mistake," reminded him again how the new drill press worked. (Juan would then realize, without anything being said, that he had given Raul incorrect instructions.)

Carl has been boorish even by American standards, but it is typical of him to have zeroed in on the task. His first thought—his instinct—is to correct the error Juan has made so that the work in this factory will proceed smoothly and production won't be disrupted. What really matters, in other words, is efficiency and not whether someone's feelings get hurt.

But is this being altogether fair to Carl (and his compatriots)? Granted, he may be just another cold, unfeeling American manager possessed of a characteristically single-minded obsession with production (and the worker be damned). But as we have noted before, Americans tend to identify very closely with their work: if our work is good, then we are good. In this context, Carl's impulse to correct Juan might very well be an expression of his instinctive concern for Juan's feelings. After all, Juan would be embarrassed if the men under him kept making mistakes and production in his division plummeted. In short, the typical American manager's obsession with output and production doesn't necessarily mean a lack of caring for the worker. If workers identify with their work, then worrying about output is synonymous with caring for the worker.

35. Calling in Sick

Ms. Parker has recently given a promotion—and is living to regret it. A good American, she chose on the basis of performance, and as Miss Lim was the most efficient worker, she naturally got the nod. And promptly came down "sick."

In her quiet way, Miss Lim is now trying to rectify the damage that has been done, which is that she has been promoted over two senior workers (who are probably older than she), both of whom have been acutely embarrassed by being passed over. By acting as if the new position is too much for her, Miss Lim is hoping to be given her old job back, thus saving the face of her two colleagues and allowing harmony to reign once again in the office.

Meanwhile, Mr. Sen and Miss Jiu are expressing their dissatisfaction in a typically indirect fashion by being even less efficient than usual. They would never approach Ms. Parker about the problem and risk further humiliation, just as Miss Lim to save her coworkers' face likewise makes no explicit reference to what has actually happened here. Notice, too, how Miss Lim manages to remain scrupulously honest throughout this encounter: when asked if the new job is too much for her, she doesn't say that it is (which would be a lie), only that it might be ("Perhaps").

At this point the alert reader might very well say: Fine. I get it. But that doesn't quite solve my problem. Miss Lim here is head and shoulders over these other two jokers and you're telling me to give one of them the job and let my business go to hell in a hand basket?

The point is well taken. The issue here isn't who's qualified and who's not (Miss Lim wins that contest hands down), but how to exploit Miss Lim's strengths without embarrassing her more modestly skilled senior colleagues. Rather than promoting Miss Lim to a higher position, she could be given the responsibility (and the reward) without the title, the office work load could be redistributed in such a way as to exploit everyone's strengths, or Miss Lim's colleagues could be given high-profile, special assignments a few weeks prior to her elevation which would, of course, preclude their availability for the position you are, as a consequence, obliged to confer on the hapless Miss Lim.

36. Choices

In general, external appearances, how one presents oneself, count for much more in Europe than they do in the United States. Indeed, they are believed to reflect the inner person—which is what makes the loud tie on the man from Oxford so genuinely troubling for Arabella. This is not to say that the British, in this instance, don't value technical expertise, but only that there are other equally important factors (such as style and manners) to look at in a job candidate.

Americans as a rule don't trust appearances. We caution against judging a book by its cover and warn that all that glitters is not gold (even as we cheerily maintain that clothes make the man). We believe, in other words, that you can—and should—distinguish between appearances and reality. This belief is no doubt the result of our fundamental conviction in the equality of all individuals, that beneath the surface we are all equally worthy. Surface appearances are, therefore, not to be trusted.

This doesn't mean, by the way, that the man from Liverpool will get the job—though it does give him an edge—but it's a good bet that if the man from Oxford is hired, a discreet hint will be planted about his ties.

37. Moving Up

Upward mobility is viewed differently in different cultures. The United States, as we've noted, is the land of rags to riches. You can start out as a clerk in the mail room and rise to CEO of the company. Where the issue is experience and proven competence—a system most often summed up in the word "meritocracy"—everyone has a shot at moving up.

In some cultures, however, the issue is experience, competence, and the right personal background. And clearly not everyone is going to qualify on all three counts. So it is that while Gaston does a good job, he would not automatically expect to move up. He might very well expect rewards for his competence and may even move up within certain limits, but he would not be a candidate for a vice presidency merely on the basis of merit. He needs to have gone to one of several universities and moved in certain social circles. Indeed, Gaston is not only sure he isn't going to become a vice president, he is actually troubled by the prospect. He knows he would not be readily received into this stratum and would therefore find it difficult to operate effectively. It's not his place.

38. Explanations

Sometime in the past, Ms. Wright explained this machine to Miss Chung and then asked her if she had understood. Miss Chung said yes. But in fact, as we now see, she had not understood and had even gone to ask her friend Li for help. Why did Miss Chung say she understood when she hadn't?

Miss Chung was trying to protect Ms. Wright from embarrassment. If she had said that she didn't understand the explanation, that would mean Ms. Wright hadn't done a very good job of explaining. And that would be humiliating for the boss. (It's also possible that Miss Chung claimed to understand in order to protect her own face and hoped her friend Li could put everything right.)

Now Miss Chung is in a tight spot: when Li can't help her, she is obliged to go back to Ms. Wright. Notice, though, how she tries to spare Ms. Wright undue embarrassment by emphasizing how complicated the machine is, implying that it must be very hard indeed to explain the workings of such a contraption.

The reader might wonder how one is supposed to find out

whether someone like Miss Chung has understood instructions. Clearly the way is not to ask a question, for the answer will have to be yes. You could ask Miss Chung to demonstrate what you have said while you watch or you could have a colleague, someone who is her peer, teach her how to use the machine.

While the issue here is one of face, it's interesting to note that Americans and (some) Asians have very different expectations of a manager, especially with regard to being able to answer technical questions put by subordinates. In one study of management behavior, respondents were asked whether they agreed with the statement: "It is important for a manager to have at hand precise answers to most questions subordinates raised about their work." Seventy-eight percent of Japanese and 73 percent of Indonesian managers agreed with the statement as against 18 percent of American managers.

39. A Software Upgrade

Brenda, like many Americans, sees change as positive; a thing is almost worth trying for no other reason than that it's new and different. "Tradition" and "traditional" may not be dirty words in our lexicon, but they are more often than not pejorative. Notice also Brenda's blithe (and very American) assumption that what's new is "bound to be better."

Russians (and most Europeans) tend to assume that what's new is automatically suspect and that, by and large, change is to be avoided except where it can't be helped (and even then it is instituted slowly and with the utmost caution). Andrei very much prefers the status quo, however imperfect it may be, to the new, which, his experience has taught him, can often be worse. He might be willing to entertain the idea of switching to the new software if there were a problem with what they are using at present, but, as Brenda cheerfully admits, there isn't. To Andrei, therefore, it looks as if Brenda wants him to make a change for no other reason than her conviction that what is new is likely to be better. Up against the tried and true, against some software that has stood the test of time, this argument doesn't stand a chance.

Beyond that, even if the new software is an improvement

over the old, would it really be worth all the time and effort required to train people in the new program? Are the new software's supposed advantages really worth the risk of disrupting productivity during the time it will take to phase it in?

The average American believes in the inexorable march of progress, that the future is bound to be better than the past. By contrast, many cultures hark back to a golden age next to which the present (to say nothing of the future) pales by comparison.

40. Writing a Report

In Ram's culture, it's the boss's job to give direction and the employee's job to please the boss. It would be presumptuous of Ram to say how long the report will take, for that would be usurping Ms. Colson's right as a boss to set deadlines. In any case, a good boss would know how long such a report should take and would specify accordingly. What's more, Ms. Colson is paid a generous salary to make decisions like this and shouldn't try to unload the responsibility onto Ram.

Ms. Colson is starting out from the point of view that employees are the best judges of their work and will perform better with minimum interference. The boss's job is to orchestrate matters so the work can be done in the time the employee says he or she needs. In short, employees are given much more responsibility for their work. One study of authority patterns in organizations in India found that 85 percent of subordinates surveyed believed they worked better under close supervision. It's hard to imagine many Americans feeling the same way.

The cultural root of Ms. Colson's attitude is probably that visceral reaction against rank, authority, and hierarchy brought to North America by the Protestants and well watered by a related bias for individualism and self-reliance. The ideal boss is still thought of as the one who gives workers their freedom and generally doesn't care what they do so long as they get the job done.

41. A Nuisance

The British are known for their understatement while Americans are known for the opposite impulse: toward directness and

exaggeration. In the situation described here, a missed deadline, an American might very well get visibly upset and not hesi-
tate to express anger or disappointment. Expecting as much,
Mary misreads Nigel's controlled, low-key response to mean that
he's not upset.

But if you begin at Nigel's starting point, that it's bad form
to state strong feelings or lose one's temper or self-control in
public, then to go so far as to say something is a nuisance actually amounts to an expression of genuine annoyance or disappointment. Then, just in case there are any lingering doubts as
to how he feels, Nigel dispels them by taking the additional step
of changing the subject, refusing to discuss the matter any further—creating, in effect, the British version of a scene. It hasn't
gone well, in short, and Nigel presumes Mary understands this.

Why this American fondness for directness—for straight talk,
straight answers, straight shooters, getting to the point and not
beating around the bush? For one thing, it's more efficient, and
we place a premium on efficiency. For another, we don't hold
saving face in such high regard as other cultures and are thus
more able to withstand the consequences of bluntness. It may
also be that our basic mistrust of words prompts us to use as few
as possible.

42. Saturday Shift

Mr. Wu isn't coming in on Saturday, as he has just explained to
Mr. Jones. Indeed, he has been making himself clear on this
point from the beginning of the exchange. The problem here is
that Mr. Wu, who is Chinese, is crediting Mr. Jones with more
subtlety (more Chinese-ness) than he is due; that is, Wu assumes
the statement that Jones is going to have to keep the production
line running on Saturday is in fact a veiled request that Wu come
in on the weekend. This is how a Chinese boss would ask the
question because to make a direct request would put the employee in the impossible position of either having to say no to
his superior—which would be very disrespectful—or of having
to say yes when he didn't want to or wasn't able to come in. If
Wu *could* come in, he would now say so unequivocally, thereby

answering the "question" that has never really been asked. But instead Wu merely says "I see," a response so far from a yes as to make it very clear (to another Chinese, at least, if not to Mr. Jones) that he's not free on Saturday. In this way he has been able to say no without ever having to use the dread word.

Mr. Jones misses the signal and now puts Wu in an impossible position with a direct question, to which Wu—above all concerned to save his boss's face—is obliged to answer yes. It's a ritualistic yes, one prescribed by the situation, and means nothing more than "I heard you." What *does* have meaning, however, and is not at all ritualistic, is the phrase "I think so" that Wu tacks on here. Wu is hedging (by giving a *qualified* yes) and thereby signaling once again that his answer is in fact no.

Mr. Jones misses the signal this time too, now forcing poor Mr. Wu to become downright blunt and announce that Saturday is his son's birthday. From Mr. Wu's vantage point this has apparently done the trick, for Mr. Jones wishes Wu and his family a nice party—meaning, Wu assumes, that he doesn't have to come in!

This is all fine and good, you may be thinking, but what if you supervise a group of Chinese (or Vietnamese) workers and want some of them to come in on Saturday? What would you do? Obviously, a direct request isn't the way to go about this. What you might do is pass the word that you wanted people to come in on Saturday and let those who could work approach you. Or you could post a sign-up sheet. As the boss, you aren't going to get no for an answer.

43. Dr. de Leon

Ms. Porter assumes the CEO will at least know something about the textile business, that one's knowledge and expertise—one's experience—are at least part of what qualifies a person for a job. But that doesn't seem to be the case in this culture, at least not at the top levels of a company. What matters here is who Dr. de Leon is, not what he knows. In a culture with a strong class system, the most important qualification for an executive position is one's personal background. Mr. Domingo makes this clear from the very beginning, when he rattles off Dr. de Leon's distinguished family name. The right name, after all, guarantees access, and access means clout. Another Latin would understand at once that we're dealing with someone of substance here.

But Ms. Porter, having just been told, now asks: "Who is he?" Mr. Domingo, no doubt taken aback, elaborates about the family to fill in the picture. Once again Ms. Porter, who evidently has a hearing problem, asks the question that's just been answered: "But what's his background?" And so on. You get the point (even if Ms. Porter does not).

44. Two New Nursing Stations

Poor Mr. Compton; he could mull this one over for months and still never understand how he ended up with two shining, new—and completely unequipped—nursing stations. He and Mr. Khouri look at the world and see two very different places. Mr. Khouri sees a dynamic, unpredictable place with very few discernible or dependable patterns; the world can't be relied upon and we can never know what the future holds. Mr. Compton sees the world as much less mysterious. To be sure, it is alive and vibrant and not altogether within our control, but for all that, it can still be objectively analyzed and its ways understood. And because we can understand the external world, we regard it as much more predictable and manageable than Mr. Khouri does.

Not long ago, Mr. Compton or someone else gave Mr. Khouri some money with the understanding that he would build a nursing station and then equip it with any funds that were left over. From Mr. Khouri's perspective, this was a dubious proposition from the outset. If money were set aside to equip the station after it was built, some two or three months from now, what guarantee was there that the money would still be there? The donor might have a change of heart in the meantime and take any unused money back; a clerk might abscond with the money; somebody might decide halfway through the project that some other project was now a priority. Anything could happen.

How much wiser it would be, then, to avoid this risk and use up all the money at once, while it was in hand, and depend on Allah's providence to provide the money for the equipment later. After all, He provided for the stations to begin with, didn't He? So Mr. Khouri built two gleaming new stations and happily emptied the coffers.

Americans on the whole are not a fatalistic people; we do not have what the great Spanish writer Miguel de Unamuno called the tragic sense of life. While we believe that external forces are real enough and can certainly intrude into our lives, ours is still a reluctant, halfhearted acceptance of the power of fate or destiny. We admit that for the moment chance may still have us baffled, but we look forward confidently to the day when we will get to the bottom of it. Meanwhile, we reserve to ourselves the ability to manipulate or bend external forces to our will, with more success sometimes than others.

This optimistic slant on human affairs comes naturally to a culture founded by people who rejected the hand fate dealt them, who refused to acquiesce in the oppressive, exploitative system the Old World imposed upon them and crossed a dangerous ocean to find better terms. Having found those terms—or created them—it's no wonder they believe so strongly in themselves. In its various manifestations, this fact, more than any other, distinguishes the Old World from the New.

45. Thumbs Down

Asians, Japanese in this instance, tend to be less individualistic than Americans; the most important unit is the group, not the individual. In cultures where the group is paramount—the work group, the family, one's classmates—harmony becomes an essential value and consensus decision making is the rule. "Until 100 years ago," John Graham and Yoshiro Sano write in their book, S*mart Bargaining: Doing Business with the Japanese,*

> ...five-sixths of the population of Japan was employed in rice cultivation. Rice production requires community effort and cooperation. Irrigation, planting and harvesting are most efficiently accomplished with the participation of groups of families. Thus the small group has evolved as the salient social unit in Japan.[2]

Jenny, from a culture where majority agreement is sufficient, finds it hard to believe that if everyone in the meeting except Mr. Takeda agreed on the proposal, it was not voted on and passed. But from Tomoko's point of view, if Mr. Takeda doesn't agree—and he would have expressed his reservations very quietly and probably before rather than during the meeting—then passing the proposal would have upset Mr. Takeda and adversely affected the harmony of the group. That, in turn, would be a more serious matter than the outcome of any one particular vote.

It's sometimes difficult for Americans to identify with consensus decision making, not only because we are an individualist culture, but because consensus decisions take a lot longer to reach (and are therefore inefficient). On the other hand, many observers have noticed that once a group reaches consensus on a matter, it tends to achieve the agreed-upon goal much more quickly. In the United States, in contrast, we may get our 51 percent without much trouble, but we often spend a lot of time later on motivating and encouraging the 49 percent who weren't convinced in the beginning. In the end, the only difference between American and Japanese decision making may be that we do our consensus building after the vote and the Japanese do it before.

46. Fourth-Quarter Sales

Gloom is relative. To a realist, an honest appraisal of an unpromising situation—what the Russian Mr. Karpov is making here—is simply being objective and doesn't have to mean that one is depressed or gloomy. To an optimist like Ms. Joseph, however, determined to put the best face on everything, an honest appraisal of a bad situation inevitably comes across as pessimism.

As a rule, Americans feel obliged to be upbeat, always to look for the silver lining. It's not normal or natural to be down; if you are down, you should see someone about it (who will, of course, be able to cure you). Naturally, then, people who see unpleasant situations for what they are often strike Americans as unnecessarily negative, even cynical. (Americans are accused of a lot of things, but cynicism isn't one of them.)

We have an especially hard time with evil; in a word, we deny it. When someone commits a particularly dastardly deed, we are at pains—indeed, we are quite anxious—to find the explanation for it, in the person's childhood, say, or in a recent catastrophe that unhinged the poor soul. When we do find the explanation (and we *always* do), then we breathe a little easier. That explains it, we say, meaning that this wasn't normal, meaning, in other words, that evil isn't resident in the human condition but an alien visitor to it.

We're a long way from Ms. Joseph and Mr. Karpov, but this is the operative ethos here. The source for American optimism, for accentuating the positive, as the old song has it, is partly that lack of fatalism noted above. If we really do have control over our destiny, then there's no excuse for being down. A related notion here is our unshakable belief in the march of progress, a conviction that the human condition can be constantly improved through individual and collective effort. And then there's the sense that ours is the land of opportunity; if we fail, we can always get back up and try again. "Our national assertion in the earliest days was that America was literally the promised land," Stuart Miller writes, and this "soaring optimism was reinforced by the founding of the Republic," followed not long after by "the settling of the vast continent, an apparently endless success story."[3]

In short, there's never any good reason to lose hope; if you do, you're just being self-indulgent. It's Huck Finn, after all, the eternal optimist, rather than Hamlet, the melancholy Dane, that Americans warm to.

47. A Call to Personnel

The issue here, from Ricardo's point of view, is the importance of respecting the chain of command, especially the need to defer to one's superiors. In this instance that means referring the decision to hire the temporary workers to Señor Ramos, the chief, for his approval. Harold is correct when he says that Señor Ramos

will only ask Ricardo what he wants to do and then agree, but
he's missing the point. It isn't so much the substance of the decision that matters, but the form. In other words, it's not a question of who knows best—everyone realizes that Ricardo does—
but of who's in charge. While going to Señor Ramos might seem
to Harold like an empty gesture—and certainly a waste of time—
to Ricardo and the chief (and anyone else who may be watching)
it is an expression (albeit ritualistic) of respect for and deference
to authority. It may all be highly symbolic, but symbols are more
real in some cultures than in others.

Naturally, Harold sees things a little differently; his priority
is not the chain of command (respecting the hierarchy) but getting these people on board so he can get the job done. If he
were in Señor Ramos's position, he would expect Ricardo to
seize the initiative and take decisive action. And he would certainly not appreciate being interrupted in the midst of sensitive
discussions with Japanese buyers.

In the United States we regard hierarchies as artificial, self-
imposed structures that are often quite convenient, and we respect them so long as they suit our purposes. But when they
stand in the way of getting the job done, we think nothing of
going around them. In one study,[4] 68 percent of American managers said they agreed with the statement that "in order to have
efficient work relationships, it is often necessary to bypass the
hierarchical line." And in a related question, managers were
asked whether they agreed with the statement that "the main
reason for a hierarchical structure is so that everybody knows
who has authority over whom." Only 18 percent of the Americans said yes.

The American attitude toward hierarchies is of a piece with
our antipathy toward rank and status. Hierarchies remind us of
class systems, where some people think they're better than others. And as we have noted elsewhere, if there's anything Americans can't abide, it's people who "put on airs," "pull rank," or
otherwise "lord it over" others. Egalitarianism is so much a part
of our culture it's become firmly embedded in idiomatic expression. There's also the problem that respecting the chain of command takes time—and that can be inefficient.

Needless to say, this attitude toward hierarchy and the chain of command can vary greatly from one organization to the next, and even within the same organization, depending on the circumstances. In the government, for example, the pecking order is closely respected, and in the military it's a way of life. But even then, it's curious how those higher up the ladder are not respected if they act superior.

48. A New Procedure

Someone has made a mistake and it needs to be corrected; on this point, Ms. Cooper and Mr. Wong would no doubt agree. Where they part company is in how the situation should be handled. Ms. Cooper wants to identify the person or persons responsible, not necessarily to reprimand or punish them but because it's probably the quickest way to solve the problem.

Mr. Wong, every bit as keen as Ms. Cooper to find out what has gone wrong, is clearly uncomfortable with the American's approach. While it may seem to be efficient, it's going to result in embarrassment and quite possibly public humiliation for one or several people, starting with Mr. Tung. And just how efficient is that? Notice how Mr. Wong tries three times to divert Ms. Cooper from her course. First, he understates the matter, referring only to "some small problems." Then, when Ms. Cooper persists, he avoids the direct question and tries to shift the discussion from the dangerous direction of what has gone wrong to the more comfortable question of what comes next ("We need to learn from this lesson"). Finally, when Ms. Cooper zeroes in on her prey and starts to name names, Wong makes the best of a bad situation by trying to depersonalize the blame.

Left to his own devices, how would Mr. Wong have handled this situation? Like Ms. Cooper, Mr. Wong's goal would have been to pinpoint the source of the problem but in such a way as not to embarrass anyone. To that end, he probably wouldn't have spearheaded the search himself (that could be threatening), but would have quietly let it be known—quite possibly to all divisions, not just Mr. Tung's—that such and such a procedure had some bugs in it and would have asked for suggestions for improvement. That would have been sufficient for appropriate division heads to jump into action and, in a similarly nonconfrontational fashion, encourage the people under them to look at their own work and find the problem. In short, no one would accuse anyone else of making mistakes; rather, individuals would be prompted to discover their mistakes on their own. They would still feel bad about their shortcomings, but they would not feel so exposed and threatened.

49. Feasibility Study

Ms. Warner wants to examine the substance of the Ministry's new project to see if it is in fact a viable proposition. Mr. Ranjit is also very interested in determining the project's viability, but not by examining its substance; he will decide based on who is put in charge of the project. That is, if someone of influence and authority is put in charge, that will be the sign that the Ministry takes the project seriously (the substance notwithstanding). Similarly, if a minor official with no particular clout is given the program, it's a good bet the enterprise will never get off the ground (once again, the substance notwithstanding).

The American's inclination is to assume that government programs are selected and/or created based on their inherent validity, that they meet some pressing national or regional need. Personalities, in other words, should not play any part in the matter; civil servants should be above subjective considerations. But Mr. Ranjit knows his country: when a pressing national need squares off against a pressing personal agenda, it's no contest. This doesn't have to mean that civil servants in India are in the game merely to advance their own selfish interests; rather it may only mean that they naively assume their own interests and those of their constituents to be one and the same. A charming conceit, you say? Ask your own congressman or congresswoman.

Endnotes

1. Lynn Payer, *Medicine and Culture* (New York: Penguin, 1988), 37.

2. John Graham and Yoshiro Sano, *Smart Bargaining: Doing Business with the Japanese* (New York: HarperCollins, 1989), 20.

3. Stuart Miller, *Understanding Europeans*, 33.

4. Andre Laurent, "The Cultural Diversity of Western Conceptions of Management," *International Studies of Management and Organization*, vol. XIII, no. 1-2 (Spring-Summer, 1983), 75-96.

4

The World of Business: Dialogues 50-74

What I say is this, and this I do not say to all Englishmen. God made us different—you and I, and your fathers and my fathers. For one thing we have different standards of honesty and speaking the truth. That is not our fault, because we are made so.... And look now what you do? You come and judge us by your own standards.

Rudyard Kipling
"East and West"

In the era of global business, cultural insensitivity is not only foolish, it's expensive. Anyone who does business overseas or would like to expand into international markets needs to be aware of how people from other cultures think and behave. Some businesspeople still try to hide behind the notion that business is a culture unto itself, often expressed in that tired formulation that "selling is selling" the world over.

Until very recently, the last thirty years or so, Americans could believe that selling was the same everywhere and not feel any ill effects. Not because that was the truth—selling has always differed from culture to culture—but because they never altered their style, and foreigners still lined up to buy, and for a very good reason: in most cases Americans were the only people offering the particular goods and services. In a sense, we didn't really sell at all in those days; customers merely bought.

Now all that has changed. There isn't a product or service we peddle that some other country doesn't also peddle, the same—or better—quality, at a competitive price, with equal or better terms. In this kind of marketplace, the seller who doesn't understand how his or her clients think doesn't stand a chance.

We're using selling here as a kind of shorthand for any business interaction. But there's much more to international business than selling, of course; there's manufacturing, service, finance, accounting, managing in overseas locations, and participating in joint ventures, to mention just a few examples of cultural interface. In each of these areas, people who have an awareness of the cultural norms and expectations of customers, employees, bosses, and colleagues will have a decided edge.

Before we plunge in, a word about organizational or corporate culture. People who work for an overseas branch of an American parent company, for example, sometimes delude themselves by thinking that Ford or Procter & Gamble function the same way the world over—same policies and standard operating procedures, same corporate strategy and long-term plan, same corporate ethos. 3M people are 3M people whether they're from St. Paul or Sao Paulo. While certain corporate attitudes and practices do transcend national boundaries, thereby creating a body of shared expectations, they only affect a small percentage of the most common interactions. As T. W. Kang has written in *Gaishi: The Foreign Company in Japan*:

> Some [foreign subsidiaries] try to operate with the same set of values as the parent company [in the U.S.]. From the American standpoint, it is natural to want a consistent value system functioning worldwide as an informal control mechanism.... But although most people I have

> met in Japanese subsidiaries say they abide by the values of their parent corporations, they usually have not internalized these values. As a result they rarely know how to apply the values in practical situations....[1]

Corporate culture, in short, is real enough, but up against national culture—in terms of impact on behavior—it comes in a distant second.

With every hope of sounding redundant, we would like to repeat here an earlier reader's advisory: You're going to meet yet another batch of insensitive Americans in this chapter—but not, you'll remember, because we think most Americans are boors or are more likely than other nationalities to be unaware, but because we have a point to bring home here.

50. A Tight Schedule

MR. ABU BAKR: Mr. Armstrong! How good to see you.

MR. ARMSTRONG: Nice to see you again, Hassan.

MR. ABU BAKR: Tell me: How have you been?

MR. ARMSTRONG: Very well, thank you. And you?

MR. ABU BAKR: Fine, fine. Allah be praised.

MR. ARMSTRONG: I really appreciate your agreeing to see me about these distribution arrangements.

MR. ABU BAKR: My pleasure. So tell me: how was your trip? Did you come direct or did you have a stopover?

MR. ARMSTRONG: No stopover this time. I'm on a tight schedule. That's why I'm so grateful you could see me on such short notice.

MR. ABU BAKR: Not at all. How is my good friend, Mr. Wilson?

MR. ARMSTRONG: Wilson? Oh, fine, fine. He's been very busy with this distribution problem also.

MR. ABU BAKR: You know, you have come at an excellent time. Tomorrow is the Prophet's birthday—blessings and peace be upon Him—and we're having a special feast at my home. I'd like you to be our guest.

MR. ARMSTRONG: Thank you very much. Now about these plans.

51. A Good Price

MS. YOUNG: We will charge you $5 per unit if you order 10,000 units.

MR. KAWABATA: That's a good price, Ms. Young.

MS. YOUNG: So you accept that price?

MR. KAWABATA: It's very good.

MS. YOUNG: Great! Let's talk about a delivery schedule then.

52. An Honorable Company

MR. WILLIAMS: We agreed the building would be completed by the middle of October.

MR. PAPAS: Yes. That's what it says in the contract.

MR. WILLIAMS: But now there's not enough time. You'll need at least two more months.

MR. PAPAS: Oh yes. At least.

MR. WILLIAMS: The only way you could finish in time is if you hire twenty-five more workers.

MR. PAPAS: Yes. There's no question. The only way we could meet the contract as it is now written is if we hire more workers.

MR. WILLIAMS: But if you hire more workers, you won't make a profit. In fact, you'll lose money.

MR. PAPAS: Very true. We can't afford to hire more workers.

MR. WILLIAMS: Then you can't possibly meet the terms of the contract.

MR. PAPAS: We must honor the contract. We are an honorable company.

53. Making A Recommendation

MS. REYNOLDS: Have you had a chance to look at our suggestions for repairing the dam?

MR. ZHANG: Yes. We've read them all with great interest.

MS. REYNOLDS: So which one have you chosen?

MR. ZHANG: My colleagues and I like #5 the best. The others are very good too, but only #5 will do what we want.

MS. REYNOLDS: So when can we start hiring contractors?

MR. ZHANG: We must first get the approval of our superior, Mr. Hu.

MS. REYNOLDS: I see. So you will recommend #5 to him?

MR. ZHANG: We will explain the situation to him and ask if he has any advice.

MS. REYNOLDS: Does he have any background in this area?

MR. ZHANG: Oh no. My colleagues and I are the technical experts.

MS. REYNOLDS: Then Mr. Hu will accept your recommendation.

MR. ZHANG: Oh, we won't be making a recommendation.

54. Caught off Guard

BEV: The August figures are in.

LATIFA: How did we do?

BEV: Pretty well, overall, but our fuel costs were one-third more than we projected, and that took quite a bite out of our profits.

LATIFA: With the rise in oil prices, what could we do?

BEV: I know. That caught us off guard. I'm going to go back and check our analysis again. Something tells me we should have seen that coming.

LATIFA: How do you mean?

55. Layoffs

HANK: We may have to lay off some people.

FRANCESCA: Yes. I think it's unavoidable.

HANK: But I want to do it as painlessly as possible.

FRANCESCA: Yes, of course.

HANK: If we let them know now, that will give them two months, until June, to look for other work.

FRANCESCA: That will be very helpful.

HANK: Then, in July, we can look at how much we're saving.

FRANCESCA: Saving?

HANK: When they go off the payroll.

FRANCESCA: But I thought you said you wanted to do this painlessly?

56. *Yamada Distributors*

MR. BROWNING: Since we have a few minutes left in our meeting, I'd like to bring up the subject of Yamada distributors.

MR. OTOMO: Yamada? What about them?

MR. BROWNING: Well, I don't think any of us are that pleased with their services. I think we should find a new distributor. I've heard that Inoue Company is quite good.

MR. OTOMO: I wonder what others think. Have you discussed this with anyone else?

MR. BROWNING: Not really. That's why I'm bringing it up now, to get your opinions.

MR. OTOMO: Yes, we should get people's opinions before we decide.

MR. BROWNING: Good. So what do you think, Otomo-san?

MR. OTOMO: I couldn't really say.

57. *The Division Chiefs Meet*

MS. THOMPSON: Have the production figures improved any since our last meeting?

MRS. THATCHER: No, no improvement since our last division chiefs' meeting, I'm afraid. There's something not quite right.

MS. THOMPSON: What do you think's going on?

MRS. THATCHER: We don't really have the full picture. We need to know more about what's going on on the shop floor.

MS. THOMPSON: That's what I thought. But now I'm not so sure that's where the problem is.

MRS. THATCHER: Why do you say that?

MS. THOMPSON: I invited several shop managers to come to this meeting today, but they said there was nothing to report.

58. Just Trying to Help

ERIC: I saw the man in the Customs Office today.

HASSAN: Oh good.

ERIC: He said you never spoke to him about releasing that shipment.

HASSAN: I'm very sorry, sir.

ERIC: In fact, he said he's never even heard of you.

HASSAN: It's possible, sir.

ERIC: But when I asked you if you knew him and could help, you said you would try.

HASSAN: Oh, yes.

ERIC: But it wasn't true. You don't know him and you didn't talk to him.

HASSAN: Excuse me, sir. But I was only trying to help.

59. L'École des Hautes Études Commerciales

M. LE BEAU: I think we have an excellent candidate for that marketing v.p. position.

MS. ROGERS: Great! Who?

M. LE BEAU: His name is Jean-Francois Bertrand.

MS. ROGERS: What are his qualifications?

M. LE BEAU: He went to l'École des Hautes Études Commerciales.

MS. ROGERS: What did he study?

M. LE BEAU: Excuse me?

MS. ROGERS: What did he specialize in?

M. LE BEAU: I'm not sure, accounting or something like that.

MS. ROGERS: But if you don't know, how can you be sure he's qualified?

60. An Idea Man

FRAULEIN BRAUN: Have you met Dr. Ulrich?

MS. BURBANK: No, but I've heard a lot about him. He's quite an intellectual, they say.

FRAULEIN BRAUN: Oh, yes. He has two doctorates, one in political science and one in engineering.

MS. BURBANK: A real idea man, then. But not much experience in operations, I've been told.

FRAULEIN BRAUN: No, very little.

MS. BURBANK: But I also heard he was the heir apparent to the top job, when Herr Muller steps down next spring.

FRAULEIN BRAUN: Yes. We're very pleased.

61. Feedback

LETICIA: What did you think of the new design?

BILL: Very nice. I'm quite pleased.

LETICIA: It's good then?

BILL: Yes. There's one drawing that needs to be worked on a little, but that's about it.

LETICIA: I see.

BILL: What about that other piece you were working on? Any chance I could see it soon?

LETICIA: We can make it a priority, if you'd like.

BILL: Great. Thanks.

LETICIA: So you want us to scrap this design then?

62. Negotiations

MARTHA: How did the negotiations go?

JANET: Not so well. We were taken.

MARTHA: What happened?

JANET: Well, I proposed our starting price, and Maruoka didn't say anything.

MARTHA: Nothing?

JANET: He just sat there, looking very serious. So then I brought the price down.

MARTHA: And?

JANET: Still nothing. But he looked a little surprised. So I brought it down to our last offer and just waited. I couldn't go any lower.

MARTHA: What did he say?

JANET: Well, he was quiet for about a minute, and then he agreed.

MARTHA: Well, at least we've got a deal. You should be pleased.

JANET: I guess so. But later I learned that he thought our first price was very generous.

63. A Promotion for Mr. Liu

MS. HART: Nice to see you again too, Mr. Sen. How's everything going?

MR. SEN: Very good, thank you. Did you hear that Mr. Liu's been promoted? He's no longer our division chief.

MS. HART: Yes. Please offer him my congratulations when you see him.

MR. SEN: Good. I will.

MS. HART: So. What can I do for you?

MR. SEN: We'll be needing to make a few alterations in the contract.

MS. HART: Alterations? But you already signed the contract.

MR. SEN: Yes, we're very happy to be working with you and look forward to a long and mutually fruitful relationship.

MS. HART: Yes, we're very pleased too.

MR. SEN: Of course. Now about these changes…

MS. HART: I'm not sure I understand. Has something happened since we reached our agreement?

64. Some New Accounts

MS. FOSTER: I had hoped we could develop some new accounts with this new software program.

COLIN DAVIES: Oh yes. I think this product will definitely help us penetrate some new markets.

MS. FOSTER: We'll be kicking off the promotion campaign by the end of next month.

COLIN DAVIES: We've already made some preliminary contacts. There's a lot of interest. We plan to make some initial visits starting week after next.

MS. FOSTER: Great! That should boost our fourth-quarter numbers a bit.

COLIN DAVIES: How do you mean?

MS. FOSTER: You know, increased sales.

COLIN DAVIES: A bit early to say, I'm afraid.

MS. FOSTER: But I thought you said there was a lot of interest?

COLIN DAVIES: Oh yes, a lot.

65. The Delivery Date

MR. CARPENTER: I'd like to come back to the question of the delivery date again. We seem to have skipped over that one.

MR. SATO: Yes. This issue is slightly complicated. It will take some thought.

MR. CARPENTER: Not really. It's just a matter of choosing a date all of us here can agree on.

MR. SATO: Yes, choosing a date.

MR. CARPENTER: I think three months after the start of production is reasonable. What do you think?

MR. SATO: Yes. Three months. Very reasonable. Perhaps we can take a break now.

MR. CARPENTER: A break? Right now? We only have this one item left and then we'll be finished. If we could just decide.

MR. SATO: Yes, we need to decide. If we could just have a break.

MR. CARPENTER: OK. But let's make it quick.

66. The Workers Speak

MS. PARKER: Efficiency is falling in the quality-control division. What can we do?

MISS RAMIREZ: The workers may have some ideas.

MS. PARKER: Good. Why don't we call a meeting and ask them.

MISS RAMIREZ: A meeting?

MS. PARKER: Yes. And I'll run it myself and let them know how much we value their input.

MISS RAMIREZ: You'll go to the meeting?

67. Other Appointments

MS. EMERY: I see what you mean. That's a very important point. But...

MRS. BIAGGI: Now if I could explain some of the details.

MS. EMERY: Why didn't you bring this up earlier?

MRS. BIAGGI: Excuse me?

MS. EMERY: I mean this is something we need to look at very closely. But I've got another...

MRS. BIAGGI: Yes, of course. Now if you will just bear with me.

MS. EMERY: Let me ask my secretary to put you on my calendar for Friday.

MRS. BIAGGI: Excuse me?

MS. EMERY: So we can continue then.

MRS. BIAGGI: You want me to come back?

68. A Funny Feeling

MICHAEL: So, Mohamed. How did we do?

MOHAMED: Mr. Malik was impressed. Your market analysis was very thorough and your presentation was clear and precise. A very balanced, objective presentation.

MICHAEL: Well, we did our homework. The statistics really tell the story; they're very convincing.

MOHAMED: Yes, there were many statistics.

MICHAEL: But I feel funny about this one. I'm not sure he's going to sign with us.

MOHAMED: I think he may have felt there was something missing, that we're not very eager for his business.

MICHAEL: I don't know what else I could have done. The facts really speak for themselves in this case.

69.　*Small Successes*

MS. THOMAS: Well, I understand your company is one of the best architectural firms in Kyoto.

MR. OHMAE: Thank you for this invitation.

MS. THOMAS: On the contrary, it's our pleasure. Now it says here you've had a very successful business for almost thirty years.

MR. OHMAE: We've had some small success, yes. Did you speak to Mr. Mizawa?

MS. THOMAS: Yes I did. He said many of your buildings have won awards.

MR. OHMAE: A few perhaps.

MS. THOMAS: And you've had a lot of experience with office buildings.

MR. OHMAE: We have designed a few.

MS. THOMAS: Can you handle a project of this size?

MR. OHMAE: We will try our very best.

MS. THOMAS: Your best? It says here you've designed several buildings twice this size.

MR. OHMAE: That's possible.

MS. THOMAS: Do you have some hesitation in taking on this project?

MR. OHMAE: Hesitation? Excuse me, but no.

70. Basics

MISS LI: And as we have said, this was all part of the vision of our founder.

MR. HOLT: I see. Well, Tsai International certainly has an interesting history. Perhaps now, if you don't mind, we could talk about how we might be able to do business together.

MISS LI: You have nothing to add?

MR. HOLT: About us? Not really. As you know, we're a pretty young company, nothing like Tsai.

MISS LI: Well, then, as you say, we can talk about doing business. With your permission, we might begin by describing for you our organizational structure and how it reflects our company principles. And then perhaps you could do the same.

MR. HOLT: I see. And then we can talk about specific terms?

MISS LI: Terms?

MR. HOLT: You know, some of the basics?

MISS LI: But we are talking about basics.

71. An Unexpected Visit

MS. GREEN: Matsumoto-san. Good to see you again.

MR. MATSUMOTO: Thank you.

MS. GREEN: How are things?

MR. MATSUMOTO: Fine. I came to tell you that our new vice president for distribution is coming in next week.

MS. GREEN: Good. Was he expected?

MR. MATSUMOTO: We just heard yesterday. We're setting up appointments for him with all our suppliers and he'd like to see you, if you have any free time, of course. We'd like you to come on Wednesday at 9:00.

MS. GREEN: Let me check my calendar. We have our regular staff meeting on Wednesday mornings, but I'm sure I can change that. Let me just check and get back to you later this morning.

MR. MATSUMOTO: I'm sorry for the trouble.

MS. GREEN: Not at all.

72. Dotting the J's

MR. CARTER: We need to nail down the export contract by the end of next week.

M. DELON: Yes.

MR. CARTER: Perhaps we could meet on Friday morning to dot the *i*'s and cross the *t*'s.

M. DELON: What about Thursday? I was planning to take a three-day weekend with the family.

MR. CARTER: We won't be ready. But why don't you go ahead anyway and just send your assistant. What's his name again?

M. DELON: La Forge?

MR. CARTER: Yes, La Forge. He'll be implementing all this anyway.

M. DELON: But he knows nothing of these negotiations.

73. Home from Osaka

HIROSHI: I understand Bob's coming back from Osaka.

CHRISTINE: Yes, we're reassigning him to New York. It's too bad, too; he's been pulling out all the stops ever since he got there last year.

HIROSHI: Is there something wrong? With his family or his health, maybe?

CHRISTINE: No. Nothing's wrong. It just hasn't worked out over there.

HIROSHI: I heard he had made some good contacts and even got a few feelers.

CHRISTINE: There's been some interest, but he says the Japanese are just being polite. There's been no real business.

74. A Good Meeting

MRS. PONTI: If you've got a few minutes, I'd like to show you around and introduce you to some other people.

MS. PRICE: No, no thank you, ma'am. I'd better be getting back to my office. They'll be wondering what happened to me.

MRS. PONTI: Well, it has been good talking to you, Ms. Price.

MS. PRICE: Yes, ma'am. I think we've had a very good meeting. I understand your situation much better now. Your explanations were very helpful.

MRS. PONTI: Yes, yes, a good meeting. We had a good talk. We like your ideas. You must visit again soon. Come anytime.

MS. PRICE: Why don't I come when we get those materials from headquarters? That shouldn't take more than a month. I'll bring them by and we'll go over them.

The World of Business: Explanatory Notes

50. A Tight Schedule

Mr. Armstrong has a rather narrow notion of what one talks about at a "business" meeting. Not wanting to use up too much of Mr. Abu Bakr's time—who has no doubt had to juggle his schedule in order to make room for Mr. Armstrong—the American comes right to the point. Or, rather, he comes right to what he thinks is the point: the question of the distribution arrangements.

But this doesn't seem to be the point so far as Mr. Abu Bakr is concerned; indeed, he seems interested in practically anything but the distribution arrangements. Clearly, the Arab is operating under another set of assumptions, chief among which seems to be that there's more to meetings than doing business. In fact, from the Arab point of view the important part of a meeting is not the business matter at hand but the personal relationship that is being established and nurtured. Business, after all, is normally conducted with people, and it is getting to know and establishing rapport with those people that is the essential foundation for a successful business undertaking. In many parts of the world, business as such will not even come up in the first meetings with prospective clients or partners.

Americans are criticized around the world for getting down to business too abruptly, for appearing to be interested only in deal making and profits and not, it is implied, in getting to know the people they're doing business with. But this isn't altogether true. We *do* get down to business rather quickly, but not because we aren't interested in the people we meet; the reason, rather, is because we feel that business and socializing should not be mixed. We're quite willing to get to know clients and colleagues *after* we've finished with business or before we start—in the evenings, say, or on the weekends.

Many cultures find this distinction we make between the professional and the personal to be unnatural. Life can't be so easily segmented or compartmentalized; it is all of a piece, with its various parts inextricably intertwined. So it is that Arabs, for example, can do business at home and take care of personal matters at work. An American child would rarely be allowed to interrupt his or her father or mother during an important business meeting, but in the Middle East or in Latin America, the child might be warmly welcomed while the meeting was either put on hold or simply continued.

51. A Good Price

Ms. Young hasn't understood the Japanese "yes," which can only be appreciated in the context of the Japanese "no," which for all practical purposes doesn't exist. No one is to be publicly embarrassed or humiliated in Japan. This is the notion of face or one's image; one's own face and that of others must at all times be preserved. Because saying no or even implying displeasure or disappointment risks humiliating the other party, they must be avoided. Needless to say, in a world where you must never say no, yes gets quite a workout. There is even a book about all this called *Never Take Yes for an Answer* (and this same phenomenon is no doubt behind the title of another best-seller, *The Japan That Can Say No*).

Instead of the offensive no, the Japanese have devised a
number of ways of not quite saying yes. Among these are: 1) to
ask a question, 2) to say they don't understand, 3) to change the
subject, 4) to say they can't answer at this time, 5) to give a con-
ditional yes, 6) to say that the question is very difficult, and 7) to
claim that this question is not within their authority to answer.
To another Japanese, not saying yes means no.

In the present instance, Mr. Kawabata doesn't want to embarrass Ms. Young by refusing her price outright, so he makes
what for him is an exceedingly unenthusiastic response—"That's
a good price"—which he fully expects Ms. Young to take for the
lukewarm answer it is. Ms. Young, of course, assumes a good
price is just that. But she does check to make sure: "So you accept that price?" And the answer ("It's very good")—as close to
an outright no as Kawabata dares come (because it's so unequivocally noncommittal)—is all the affirmation Young needs.

In their book *Going International*, Copeland and Griggs write
of a banker in Tokyo who was asked by one of his employees:
"What does 'maybe' mean in English? I know what it means in
Japanese—it means no—but what does it mean in English?"[2]

But how, then, you might ask, is one to know when the Japanese are just being polite and when they have actually accepted
an offer? It's not difficult; if they have accepted an offer, then
the conversation will naturally shift to a discussion of the imple-
mentation details (of delivery or production or whatever). Conversely, if they have not accepted an offer and you move on to
discuss such details, the Japanese will come back to the unre-
solved issue at hand. If we lingered a little longer in the room
with Ms. Young and Mr. Kawabata, we would probably hear
something like the following:

MR. KAWABATA: We are quite eager to do business
with you, Ms. Young.

MS. YOUNG: Likewise, I'm sure. Now about a
delivery date...

MR. KAWABATA: And we think your product is very good.

MS. YOUNG: Thank you.

MR. KAWABATA: And your price is not too far from
what we would like to pay.

52. An Honorable Company

Some time ago Mr. Papas gave his word—in writing—he would put up a certain building by the middle of October. Now it appears that if he's going to meet his deadline, Mr. Papas will have to hire more workers and take a loss on the project. Consequently, he is looking for an honorable way out of the dilemma and has come to talk to Mr. Williams.

Mr. Papas hints rather broadly that if the contract for this building could somehow be modified, this would save him a lot of money. But he does not suggest this action himself, for that would be tantamount to admitting that he is not as good as his word. If Mr. Williams made the suggestion, however, Papas would agree in a moment, for then he could always claim that he was prepared to meet his obligations but that Williams offered to change the contract.

Indeed, if Williams doesn't pick up on the hints and offer to bail the builder out, then Papas will honor his promises, hire more workers, finish the building on time—and take a substantial loss. But even that loss would be preferable to the damage his reputation (hence, his business) would sustain if it became known that Papas & Sons Inc. was not always true to its word.

For his part, Williams no doubt senses that Papas wants to change the contract but probably does not realize that it's crucial that he (Williams) make the suggestion. Indeed, it probably seems to him like splitting hairs.

53. Making a Recommendation

To make a recommendation to someone often implies that you know more about a given matter than the other person does, which is certainly the case here with Mr. Zhang and his colleagues who, by their own admission, are the technical experts. So what's the problem?

The problem is that Mr. Hu is Zhang's superior, and subordinates should always defer to and otherwise show respect for their superior. In this instance that means not implying that they know more than their superior by being so bold as to make a recommendation. Instead, they will "explain the situation to [Mr.

Hu] and ask if he has any advice." At which point, Mr. Hu will no doubt ask Zhang et al. what they think, listen politely, and choose the course of action clearly preferred by the experts (who will slant their presentation accordingly).

To Ms. Reynolds this will no doubt seem like so much posturing and playacting, an empty gesture for the sake of an old man's pride. But in that very formulation lie several of the key differences between East and West: the relative values placed on form (as opposed to content), age, and personal honor.

54. Caught off Guard

Bev believes the world is essentially a predictable place, that it operates according to certain laws and patterns, and that those laws and patterns, once pinned down and figured out, will always hold true. If something unexpected happens, it's not because the world is capricious and arbitrary, but because one didn't read the signs well enough. In other words, there's a reason or an explanation for why things happen the way they do, and one can know those reasons if one but takes the trouble.

Latifa, who is an Arab, believes there's a reason too, a very definite pattern or plan in the way events unfold, but she does not feel that people can know it. They're welcome to try, of course, and may even figure out a few minor patterns here and there, but there is much that will ultimately remain unknowable. This is not to say that we shouldn't plan for the future or try to take matters into our own hands, only that we shouldn't become too fond of our plans or too sure of our hands.

Thus it is that Bev instinctively believes the problem is either in her data or in her analysis, but not in external events she couldn't fathom or foresee. To Latifa, the notion of being able to see what is coming, as Bev puts it, is a veritable contradiction in terms; what has not yet come cannot be seen.

The moral of the story is that if you're a seismologist, you'll find employment more readily in the United States than in Abu Dhabi, the incidence of earthquakes notwithstanding.

55. Layoffs

What is an employer's responsibility to his or her employees? In some cultures the employer-employee relationship is largely opportunistic: employees take a job, do their best, and keep an eye open for advancement—in that company or in any other company where there might be an opportunity. And when they find their chance, they take it and no one feels used. For their part, meanwhile, employers are glad for the services of employees, pay them well, train and promote them where appropriate but are not reluctant to lay them off if that becomes necessary. There is not much loyalty from either side nor anything more than what we would call a business relationship.

In Francesca's culture, the employer-employee relationship is closer and more personal. Companies look after their employees the way families look after their members and, in turn, they expect the kind of loyalty and support that family members give each other. The bond between the worker and the company is deep and lasting, with each side feeling responsible for the welfare of the other.

Francesca is thus pleased that Hank wants to treat the people who must be laid off humanely, like a caring parent. But Hank turns out not to be so caring after all, for he plans to lay these workers off and stop paying them whether they have found other jobs or not. To Francesca, this kind of treatment is no way to repay the employees' loyalty and years of dedication. They should either be kept on until they are able to find work elsewhere or, if they must be let go, paid something (or otherwise looked after) until they do find new employment. After all, they are family.

56. Yamada Distributors

Mr. Browning has caught his colleagues off guard. As a rule, the Japanese do not like to be surprised at meetings, especially if the surprise involves making a public statement of your views when you don't yet know the views of others. In a society where decisions are made by consensus, one learns to keep one's views to oneself until one sees which way the wind is blowing. If you voice a strong opinion, for example, only to learn later that yours is a decidedly minority view, you risk losing face by having to modify your position.

To Mr. Browning this is a simple matter of comparing the relative merits of the two distributors in question and picking the best one. But for the Japanese there are other issues at stake here; sooner or later it's going to come down to questions of face and honor, which means the entire discussion must be handled with the utmost delicacy. There is, for example, the rather sensitive issue of who recommended Yamada to this company to begin with and whether that person will be shamed if Yamada is now dropped. Then there's the question of who is pushing Inoue and whether that person will be embarrassed if the group decides against Inoue. And what if that person happens to be the boss or someone else quite senior? No Japanese is going to *have* an opinion on this matter—much less reveal it publicly—before knowing and carefully weighing the answers to these questions and engaging in numerous behind-the-scenes discussions. Mr. Otomo means it when he tells Mr. Browning that he can't say what his views are yet.

We might also mention here the much vaunted Japanese tradition of *keiretsu,* an interlocking network of relationships between manufacturers, suppliers, distributors, etc., which is carefully constructed and nurtured for the mutual benefit of all parties. When you change one player in a keiretsu, the whole structure is affected. Accordingly, finding a new distributor is not something that is done on the spur of the moment or without consulting one's network.

57. The Division Chiefs Meet

Ms. Thompson, the American, has a poorly developed appreciation of rank and status. This is a division chiefs' meeting in England. People from the shop floor, in this case, floor managers, aren't used to being asked to division chief meetings—and division chiefs, English ones anyway, aren't used to seeing them there. Neither would know quite what to do in the other's presence. While it would be quite appropriate and normal for a division chief to consult with a floor manager one-on-one or to meet with all his floor managers, to mix the two groups in the same meeting isn't done.

In all likelihood, the floor managers do have something to report, but they are quite uncomfortable about being invited to this particular meeting. Not wanting to be impolite when Ms. Thompson asks, they say they have nothing to report rather than refuse her invitation.

There's a division between the rank and file and middle management in America too, but it is not so wide. On the whole, ours is a more democratic and participatory workplace, where the chain of command is less sacrosanct and the hierarchy is bypassed wherever it's more efficient to do so.

58. Just Trying to Help

Raised as he was, Hassan is obliged to give a positive response to a request for help from his boss (or any close friend or associate, for that matter)—whether or not he can actually be of any real service. What Eric would call "the truth" matters much less here than good manners, which dictate that one should always indicate one's willingness to do what one can for a friend. Another Arab would know that Hassan's offer shouldn't necessarily be interpreted literally—that he actually knows the man in customs and is going to be able to do something—but rather as an indication that he is willing to try. To refuse to help, even to say that one didn't see how one could be of any help, would be rude and inhospitable. Moreover, how does Hassan know that he can't be of help? To be sure, he knows he doesn't know the man in the Customs Office, but maybe a friend of his or someone in his family does. There's always a chance, in other words, that one will be able to do something, and so long as that chance exists, however remote, there's no need to insult a friend by not acting hospitably.

It gets worse. From his perspective, Hassan expects Eric will wait a decent interval to see if anything comes of this offer of assistance, and if nothing does, then he expects Eric will realize that he (Hassan) was unable to do anything and will look for a

solution elsewhere. Instead, Eric confronts Hassan with his fail-
ure, which is very embarrassing, and even calls him a liar. It's a
measure of Hassan's good manners that he keeps his cool and
apologizes even as his honor is being dragged through the mud.

59. L'École des Hautes Études Commerciales

If you've been to l'École des Hautes Études, it doesn't matter
what you studied; you're qualified. Qualified, that is, to take
over a senior position in a French company where what matters
is not so much what one knows—what one studied or one's technical qualifications—but one's personal background and social
pedigree, what circles one travels in. At this level in a company,
it is manners and connections that determine how accepted—
hence, how effective—one will be. At lower levels, one's skills
and training are important, but not so when one is near the top.

The United States, of course, is a supposed meritocracy,
where one advances according to one's wits and abilities—the
whole notion behind that quintessentially American phenomenon of the self-made man or woman. In Europe, Stuart Miller
points out, "...the self-made man has money, but he should have
something more: he should bear the traditional marks of a high
person and, because he made himself, he doesn't. He has been
rough, rude, pushing himself forward and he remains rude, out
of place in a preformed scheme.... No European I have ever
met could fully understand or accept the fact that in the United
States even an actor can be elected President."[3]

We're talking here, of course, about the class system, which
most Americans have an instinctive reaction to, for it seems to
mean that certain people, by the mere accident of birth, are
better than other people. While some lords and ladies may have
once behaved that way (thus driving our forebears to the boats),
and while some others no doubt carry on this dubious tradition
even today, this is not the true meaning of class in Europe. It's
not that someone who went to l'École des Hautes Études thinks
he or she is necessarily better than or superior to someone who
didn't (or who went to none at all), and it is even less the case
that the unschooled feel outclassed by the high and the mighty.

The point is, rather, that different life circumstances prepare you for different paths—each one, by the way, just as honorable as the next—and it's silly to act as if they didn't. It's not so much the nature of one's station in life that matters but what one does with one's potential. An expert plumber feels every bit the equal of a member of parliament, and an M.P. knows better than to condescend to his plumbing constituents. True class, in short, is not a function of birth; the highborn and the lowborn can both be boorish and classy in their turn.

60. An Idea Man

We have here another manifestation of the American attitude toward ideas and intellectuals. Americans tend to be of two minds about ideas: we have a certain respect for them, much the same way we value education, but just as we don't value education for its own sake—it's only a means to an end—so ideas in and of themselves don't impress us. Show me the practical application of an idea—how I might make some money from it—and then I start to get interested.

So it is that Ms. Burbank can't quite figure how the Germans can pick Dr. Ulrich to run their company. He'd be fine up in R and D or off in some think tank, but running the organization when he doesn't know anything about operations? For the Germans, and most Europeans, ideas and knowledge are greatly respected; they have a certain weight and value all their own. The development of the mind and the refinement of the intellect are worthy ends in themselves, the sign of a well-rounded individual. Someone with a thorough education is likely to have the vision and understanding necessary to run a company or, for that matter, to succeed in any task he or she undertakes. He or she may not be much of a manager, but that's not important at the top of a company; what matters in that rarefied atmosphere is someone with vision and a discerning intellect.

By and large, Americans are anti-intellectual (which most of us cheerfully admit). We think ideas for their own sake are fine—on university campuses, which is, not surprisingly, the same place that gave us those other two dubious distinctions, the ivory tower and the absentminded professor. Ideas, at least abstract ones, don't engage us, probably because they are too far removed from concrete achievements, our real heroes. It's probably no coincidence that there are no great American philosophers, with the possible exception of William James (whose most lasting contribution, interestingly enough, was the theory of pragmatism!).

61. Feedback

Latins are inclined to be indirect so as not to embarrass one another. Criticism, accordingly, has to be handled with the utmost delicacy and in any case must never appear to be what it is. In practice, critical comments usually come in the guise of faint or insufficient praise or as outright avoidance of the touchy subject. In either case Latins, with their heightened sensitivity in this regard, note the critical omission and get the intended message, which is what Leticia thinks she is getting here.

When Bill makes only one reference (albeit positive) to the new design, Leticia is immediately suspicious. Even then she checks out this impression by asking Bill if the design is good—and knows there's trouble when Bill cites a minor problem. As if this weren't enough, Bill then drops the subject entirely and brings up another one, proof positive to Leticia that Bill is very displeased with the new design. At which point, Leticia naturally offers to junk the new design altogether.

Bill's mistake, clearly, was not to be effusive in his praise. In a culture where faint praise is damning, slightly exaggerated praise is simply the norm. Most Americans, given to directness, are suspicious of effusive praise (except where clearly warranted) and take faint praise for nothing more (or less) than what it is. We don't read between the lines, in other words, because we usually say what we mean in the lines themselves—and expect everyone else to.

62. Negotiations

Speech, the Japanese say, is silver, but silence is golden. Americans are uncomfortable with periods of silence in conversation;

we rush to fill any void longer than five seconds. We think silences mean the other person hasn't understood or that things aren't going well—that the other person is upset, not pleased, or just not interested. The Japanese believe it is polite not to respond immediately after someone has spoken, especially if that person has made a proposal of some sort or other. A pause of up to thirty seconds before answering shows respect to the speaker, indicating that one is carefully considering what one has heard and is carefully composing one's reply. An immediate response betrays a person who is not careful or reflective, a dubious business partner.

In the present case, Janet assumed Mr. Maruoka's silence meant displeasure or disappointment, and she lowered her price in response, only to be met with silence again. Mr. Maruoka, meanwhile, can scarcely believe his good fortune.

63. A Promotion for Mr. Liu

For Americans, the foundation of a business undertaking is a signed contract which spells out all the mutually agreed-upon details of the relationship. It's neat and clean, we say, meaning it keeps everything on a more objective, impersonal level. People may come and go, but the contract will endure.

For the Chinese, the foundation of a business undertaking is the rapport and trust—the personal relationship—that is established between the two parties during any number of preliminary meetings. A signed contract may well follow from such a process, but it is merely a formality, a symbol of the relationship, not the essence. Moreover, a contract is bound to change from time to time because of changed circumstances, but if the relationship is sound, such changes won't matter. As they say in Chinese, it's neat and clean.

Seen in this context, what Ms. Hart has perceived as a throwaway line, that Mr. Liu has been promoted, is in fact the key piece of information in this exchange. Now that Mr. Liu has moved on, there is a new division chief who no doubt has his own ideas about this contract—which brings us to Mr. Sen's visit today.

Ms. Hart misses the point about Liu's promotion and takes

the American position that a deal is a deal; it's all in writing. It is indeed in writing, Mr. Sen maintains, but now some additional writing is called for. But what should that matter between trusted friends? This time it is we who want to make the change; next time it may be you. So long as we trust each other, so long as we are both committed to a long-term, mutually fruitful relationship, what are a few changes in a contract?

The American assumption here once again is that the role of external events (circumstances) can be limited, in this instance by the power of a contract. Not that we aren't willing to renegotiate a contract, but this must be done for a very good reason and a mere change in personnel hardly qualifies. For their part, the Chinese don't change contracts at the drop of a hat either. But much more than a hat has fallen here.

64. Some New Accounts

Americans sell products; the British buy reputations—and the former proceeds rather more quickly than the latter. Thus it is that Ms. Foster is perplexed to hear that the time between an initial contact and a sale should be so long. She assumes, in fact, that the sale should be the very next step, accomplished in the very next meeting. What else is there to do, after all? You've made the contact; either they like the product or they don't. If they like it, they'll place an order; if they don't, they won't.

But in England there's more to sales than just having a good product. What about the company, for example? What kind of people are these? Can they be relied upon? What is their track record? Will they follow through if something goes wrong? Can they fill a rush order if I should suddenly need one? Are they committed to the U.K. market? Do they plan to stay here for the long term? And most importantly, does anybody I know know these people?

Potential buyers need to be satisfied about these intangible, subjective factors as much as they need to be sold on the product. While you can size up a product rather quickly, the answers to questions about what kind of people these are can't be resolved in one or two meetings. The sales reps will have to court these buyers over an extended period and may very well bring them by the factory now and again to meet key people. In time, the character of these people, hence the reliability of the company, will become clear, and when it does Ms. Foster will either have her new markets or she won't. (And if she does have them, these will be customers who, thanks to this careful selection process, will buy in for the long term, who won't change suppliers at the first sign of a sweeter deal elsewhere.)

65. The Delivery Date

Mr. Carpenter is missing the point about breaks: the Japanese, eager to avoid public displays of disagreement, frequently use breaks to work out compromises on issues where the two sides are far apart. Once some middle ground is established, these no-longer-sensitive issues can then be brought back to the formal, public setting for speedy resolution with the requisite smiles all around.

While Mr. Carpenter can be forgiven for not knowing this about the Japanese, he is given several hints of Mr. Sato's reluctance to discuss delivery dates at this time—all of which he misses. The first and most obvious (which would have more than sufficed were Mr. Carpenter a fellow Japanese) is when Mr. Sato says that this is "a slightly [read very] complicated issue" that will "take some thought." As people don't normally think in public, this is a signal that the subject is not appropriate for open discussion at this time. Since Mr. Carpenter does not propose postponing the discussion, Mr. Sato now tries another tactic: stalling. While it might not seem like stalling to Mr. Carpenter, when Mr. Sato, in his next two comments, simply repeats the terms Carpenter offers without actually accepting them, this is an indication that Sato doesn't want to discuss the matter at this time.

When he couples the stalling maneuver with the first suggestion of a break, Sato-san is further signaling his discomfort with the way the conversation is going. In the end, he is as direct as he can be when he says, "Yes, we need to decide. If we could just have a break." Imagine his surprise when Mr. Carpenter—

who is, after all, the one pushing for this discussion—then suggests that the break be short!

The American habit of directness guarantees that disagreements, whether private or public, aren't the end of the world; the worst that can happen is ruffled feathers. In any case, it never hurts to clear the air. In some cultures, however, the air is perpetually charged.

66. *The Workers Speak*

This is our old friend, the concept of face, showing up in yet another guise. Ms. Parker wants to get to the bottom of things, and as quickly as possible. That means going directly to the workers in quality control and asking for their ideas.

Miss Ramirez knows this won't work and delicately tries to make this point (she must be delicate because this is her boss, and the ideas of one's boss are inevitably quite shrewd). Miss Ramirez first questions the idea of having a meeting because she knows the workers will be reluctant to present their suggestions—a suggestion, after all, is an implicit kind of criticism—in such a public setting. When Ms. Parker then goes on to state that she will chair the meeting herself, Miss Ramirez is even more surprised, for she knows that even if the workers could get up the courage to criticize the company in public, they certainly wouldn't do it to the boss's face.

Once again, notice how Miss Ramirez, ever the correct subordinate, doesn't directly deflate Ms. Parker's crazy notion but merely tosses it back to her for further reflection ("You'll go to the meeting?"), which then allows the boss to make the right decision seemingly all on her own. If Ms. Parker comes out of this looking good, Miss Ramirez comes out looking even better: not only has she saved the boss from herself, she's done it so quietly that no one will ever know—except for Ms. Parker, of course, who will no doubt express her gratitude in a suitable and most satisfying manner. (The irony here is that Ms. Parker, unlike a Spanish boss, has probably missed most of this, and Miss Ramirez may wait in vain for some sign of her boss's gratitude.)

67. Other Appointments

Many Americans are slaves to their schedules. Even though we may grudgingly admit that schedules are originally man-made, once something gets put on a schedule, it's the person—not the schedule—that has to do the accommodating. It's not that we are enamored of schedules per se, but rather of what they represent: the careful ordering and taming of external reality (which we find extremely comforting). Americans, as we've observed already, do not have a well-developed sense of limits; there's almost nothing we'll admit we can't control, including time itself.

This is why it is so difficult for Ms. Emery, against all other logic, to let Mrs. Biaggi continue with her presentation, even as Ms. Emery herself cheerfully admits that now they're gettting somewhere. Ms. Emery is clearly convinced that whatever the benefits of hearing Mrs. Biaggi out, of resolving the issue at hand and completing an important piece of business, they're bound to be outweighed by the benefits of staying on schedule. To be sure, Ms. Emery has one or two qualms ("Why didn't you bring this up earlier?"), but in the end she decides that the chaos that threatens should she abandon her schedule is not worth the gamble.

For her part, Mrs. Biaggi, operating according to another set of assumptions—which says that time and schedules are meant for one's convenience, not vice versa—is completely taken aback. What can a few minutes, even half an hour, of another person's time be worth compared to the successful completion of this transaction?

To test how important time and schedules are in a given culture, try to change a plan or an appointment at the last minute. In some countries (including the United States) one feels obliged to apologize for changing an appointment any less than a day in advance; in other cultures, you can change or cancel an appointment up to an hour beforehand without making excuses. Another sign of how important schedules are in a culture is the definition of "late." In the United States, late is ten minutes after the appointed time. If you're going to be later than this you must call or, if you can't, you must at least apologize and offer an explanation when you do arrive. In many other cultures

(Mediterranean or Hispanic, for instance), late is forty-five minutes to an hour after the appointed time. If you arrive earlier than that, there is no need to explain or apologize, for no one has been inconvenienced.

68. A Funny Feeling

Most Americans like cold, hard facts—the colder and harder the better. After all, you can't argue with the facts, with what we like to call objective reality. This is what Michael means about the facts speaking for themselves; a person can always have his or her own agenda, but statistics—the purest sort of facts—don't lie. Thus we feel that in making a presentation, if we stick to the numbers—if we are scrupulously impersonal—we can't go wrong.

Mr. Malik, however, was evidently hoping for something more. He appreciates facts, too, but he's not going to be doing business with facts; he's going to be doing business with Michael. This man, Malik is thinking, certainly seems to have his numbers right and has indeed made a compelling case for hiring someone with his expertise and savvy. But who is *he?* In addition to the facts—to what Mohamed calls Michael's "balanced, objective presentation"—Malik would like some unbalanced, subjective emotion from Michael, some indication that there's a human being in there. Mr. Malik would like to have a good feeling about Michael, but he hasn't really come out from behind his numbers.

In one sense, Michael is right. The facts do speak for themselves, which is fine as far as it goes. But who, then, speaks for him? This is what is missing in his presentation, a sense of the person and company behind the data. In the end it is the company and its people Mr. Malik is hiring and depending on, not numbers, however accurate.

Americans don't like it when someone comes on too strong in making a presentation; we become suspicious. If this guy's good, his work will speak for itself. Arabs, on the other hand, like a strong pitch, with plenty of exaggeration and enthusiasm. Without a little hyperbole, how do we know you're serious?

69. *Small Successes*

Americans see an interview as an exercise in persuasion. If you don't sing your praises or at least point out your strengths, then you either aren't interested in or qualified for the position or contract. If you don't make your case, how can the interviewer know that you're qualified? In many cultures, however, the presumption is just the opposite: if you *have* to make your case, how *can* you be qualified?

In Japan, for example, an interview is often a formality, the occasion to validate a decision that has already been made or to verify that the person selected doesn't have homicidal tendencies or orange juice on his lapel. Frequently, you will not get to the interview stage in a business undertaking unless it has been determined—through third parties—that you are essentially fit for the job. And when you do get to the interview, protocol requires that you understate your qualifications and accomplishments. It is not proper to praise yourself (or, incidentally, to put down the competition).

In this particular case, Mr. Ohmae is getting increasingly uncomfortable as Ms. Thomas keeps pressing him to blow his own horn. As Ohmae continues to resist the openings, she begins to wonder if he really wants the job or is even up to it. The most significant comment in the dialogue is Mr. Ohmae's asking Ms. Thomas if she has talked to Mr. Mizawa. If she has—and Mizawa-san has done his job properly—then Mizawa will have filled Thomas in on all of Ohmae's achievements and capabilities. And by Japanese reckoning, if Ms. Thomas has asked to see Mr. Ohmae, then it means she was satisfied from Mizawa that Ohmae is eminently qualified. To press Ohmae on this point is, in fact, to suggest that maybe Mizawa didn't altogether convince Ms. Thomas and now she is having to find out on her own.

All this is not to say that Americans don't value modesty and humility (though we don't normally expect them in an interview). We do admire the unassuming heroes and heroines who go quietly about their affairs and shun the limelight (the Gary Coopers and Jimmy Stewarts), and we likewise wince at self-promoters who cross the line between healthy self-respect and genuine conceit. In an American context, Mr. Ohmae would have presented his portfolio; in Japan that is not expected or necessary.

70. Basics

The Chinese are looking for a business partner here, which is to say a company with whom they will enter into a long-term relationship that over time will bring many years of profit to both parties. Because a great deal of time, money, and effort will be committed to this relationship (if it's going to work), the Chinese have to be satisfied as to the essential integrity and compatibility of the prospective partner. What is the history of the company and its corporate philosophy? What was the vision of the people who founded it? What are its guiding principles, its organizational approach, and its key policies? In short, will this marriage last? Depending on the answers to these questions, Miss Li and her colleagues will know what the prospects are for the kind of solid, enduring relationship they seek. To the Chinese, therefore, these rather abstract issues are the essential foundation for any kind of agreement, what they would call the basics.

Naturally, then, it is a bit unsettling for Miss Li when the Americans don't reciprocate with a history of their company, however young it may be, and likewise seem anxious to skip over the important questions and move to the minor details. Are they hiding something? Why don't they ask more questions about us?

But the Americans, under Mr. Holt, have something quicker in mind here. Their eye is less on an enduring relationship than on short-term profits, meaning that from their point of view this partnership only has to endure long enough to allow both sides to recoup their investment and make a nice piece of change. To that end, it doesn't really matter what the vision of Tsai International is or what the founder ate for breakfast. It's not that Mr. Holt has anything against a long-term, mutually satisfying relationship—if one should develop, so much the better—but it's not necessary for doing business and is therefore not a goal in these discussions.

Nor do we mean to say that the Chinese don't care about short-term profit. In fact, they feel about it much the same way

Mr. Holt does about an enduring relationship: if it should happen, so much the better, but it's not the objective. The Chinese, as we have said, are more interested in gradual, sustained growth over the long term, which is quite likely, in their view, to be more profitable than a few very good years up front. While Americans believe in seizing opportunities, the Chinese believe in creating them.

71. An Unexpected Visit

Ms. Green doesn't seem to have a very keen understanding of rank. When the vice president comes to town, all bets are off; that is, schedules get changed, rush jobs get put on hold, and immutable deadlines get muted. Mr. Matsumoto expects Ms. Green will move heaven and earth to clear her calendar for such an important visitor. Being Japanese, he makes a brief concession to politeness—"he'd like to see you, if you have any free time"—but he follows up at once with the appointment time (Wednesday at 9:00).

Imagine his surprise (one could as well imagine some other emotions) when Ms. Green suggests that she must first check her calendar. Who else on her calendar could be more important than the vice president for distribution of a major client? (And even if there were such a person, how rude to suggest such a thing!) As if that weren't bad enough, Ms. Green then suggests that the appointment conflicts with a weekly staff meeting. Not some special, once-a-year event but a routine meeting that could easily be rescheduled. While she does seem willing to change the meeting, to have even mentioned it is a mistake, for now Mr. Matsumoto knows he is causing her some inconvenience for which he is most embarrassed and apologetic.

The last straw here is when Ms. Green doesn't even make the necessary changes in her schedule on the spot, but promises to "check and get back to [Matsumoto] later." This lack of responsiveness is one final insult to Mr. Matsumoto and his boss.

What can we say in Ms. Green's defense here? She is clearly very fond of her schedule, a common trait among monochronic Americans who see a schedule as a structure into which we plug

125

people. The Japanese, on the other hand, see people as something around which one arranges schedules. Another reason for the American love affair with schedules is that they allow us to divide up our day into achievements, more or less guaranteeing that we will finish one thing (an achievement) before we start another—all of which is most gratifying.

72. Dotting the J's

French companies tend to be highly hierarchic, with little communication from one level to the next. Geert Hofstede, the Dutch sociologist, talks about low and high power-distance cultures, which vary according to how the issue of inequality is handled in a given society or group and the corresponding degree to which power is shared and authority emphasized. In high power-distance cultures, like France, much is made of power and authority, and dominance is stressed. We are not all equals here, the French believe; there are those who decide things and those who implement them. Managers tend to emphasize the distance between themselves and subordinates. And, on the whole, everyone agrees that this works just fine.

M. Delon is thus taken aback by Mr. Carter's suggestion that he should go ahead and take his three-day weekend and just send his assistant La Forge in his place. La Forge, as a subordinate, has not been privy to the high-level negotiations that are M. Delon's special province. He would not expect to be involved in decision making at this level, even though he will eventually be charged with carrying out whatever decisions are made.

73. Home from Osaka

Hiroshi is puzzled; Bob's been in Osaka less than a year and already he has made contacts and even gotten feelers. This is remarkable. If he's being called back, then the explanation can't have anything to do with his performance; it must be either a family problem or a health problem.

Christine, meanwhile, is fit to be tied. Bob's been in Osaka nearly a year and all he's got to show for it are a few contacts and the odd feeler. This train is going nowhere.

A Japanese company once sent one of its employees to San Francisco with the assignment to assess the prospects for opening up an American branch. He was told that for the first year he should simply listen and observe the local scene, not make any contacts or even rent office space.

Americans, because of their achievement orientation, want results—especially concrete results—and they want them sooner rather than later. While Hiroshi considers contacts and feelers to be significant results, they represent little to Christine, who is thinking along the lines of contracts and profits. And while a year is a long time to Christine, it's inconsequential to the Japanese. The advice given to American companies who want to enter the Japanese market is to be prepared to wait five to ten years for a return on their investment. Most American executives would have made two or three job—maybe even company—changes in that time.

74. A Good Meeting

With this dialogue, we return to where we started in this section, not so much for the sake of completing the circle but to emphasize once again how differently different cultures view and conduct business. For Ms. Price, business is clearly meetings, exchanging information, reaching agreements—all those tasks generally associated with achieving concrete, measurable results. Mrs. Ponti, however, has a broader notion of what business involves. It includes those things dear to Ms. Price, but it also includes establishing a personal relationship with one's potential associates. Indeed, from Mrs. Ponti's point of view, this personal relationship has to come first so that it can then serve as the foundation for a successful business relationship.

Notice how Mrs. Ponti refers to this encounter as a good talk (Ms. Price calls it only a meeting), asks Ms. Price to "visit" again, to come anytime, and wants to show her around and introduce her to people. She wants Ms. Price to get to know the people and the organization, assuming that until she does, she won't know whether she wants to do business with this company. At least, that's how Mrs. Ponti intends to proceed: she will get to know Ms. Price before she decides whether to do business with her. But Ms. Price doesn't seem interested in visiting—what would that accomplish? She will only be coming back when there's more business to conduct, when the materials arrive from headquarters.

As we have said, this separation of the professional and the personal—between business and pleasure—is very American. It's not that we aren't interested in getting to know the people we work with; it's just that we don't see it as a necessary part of doing business. We're happy to meet people after work, to do things on the weekend, but that shouldn't interfere with—or even affect—the business we do together. We are able to separate the person from the work.

In many other cultures, this distinction is seen as artificial at best and bad business at worst. After all, one does business with and through people, so how can you separate one from the other? Why would you take the risk of doing business with someone you didn't know and weren't sure you could trust? If there's no rapport or personal bond, what is there to sustain the business relationship, especially in difficult periods?

Endnotes

1. T. W. Kang, *Gaishi: The Foreign Company in Japan* (New York: Basic Books, 1990), 140.
2. Lennie Copeland and Lewis Griggs, *Going International* (New York: Penguin, 1985), 105.
3. Stuart Miller, *Understanding Europeans*, 100.

5

Seven Lessons

We learn from experience that not everything which is incredible is untrue.

Cardinal de Retz

There's every chance you'll emerge from these dialogues a bit rattled, humbled, and perhaps even taken aback by the workings and power of culture. And a good thing that is, too, for the central message here, after all, is that in dealing with people unlike us we can't afford to be too sure of ourselves.

This general truth can be subdivided into several lesser ones, pieces of practical advice to keep in mind when communicating across cultures. We offer these seven lessons as a kind of summing up of the notion that is at the heart of this book and is likewise the key to successful intercultural communication.

Lesson One

Don't assume sameness. We all do it all the time, of course. Indeed, we have to or it would be hard to function in the world.

Nevertheless, when you go abroad or meet people from abroad, try to entertain the notion that they might be very different from you. If it turns out they aren't, all the better; and if it turns out they are, score one for your side.

Lesson Two

What you think of as normal or human behavior may only be cultural. A lot of behavior *is* universal, of course, and doesn't differ from country to country. But not all. Before you project your norms onto the human race, consider that you might be wrong.

Lesson Three

Familiar behaviors may have different meanings. The same behavior—saying yes, for example—can exist in different cultures and not mean the same thing. Just because you've *recognized* a given behavior, don't assume you have therefore *understood* it.

Lesson Four

Don't assume that what you meant is what was understood. You can be sure of what you mean when you say something, but you can't be sure how this is understood by someone else. Check for signs that the other person did or did not understand you.

Lesson Five

Don't assume that what you understood is what was meant. You are obliged to hear what others say through the medium of your own experience. You know what those words normally mean, but whose norms are we following here: yours or the foreigner's? If they're the foreigner's, do you know what they are?

Lesson Six

You don't have to like or accept "different" behavior, but you should try to understand where it comes from. You may never get used to some of the things foreigners do (even as they are occasionally put off by you), but it can't hurt to try to figure out why they behave in such irritating ways. Once you realize, for example, that the reason Hispanics use go-betweens is because they don't want to hurt your feelings, you may be able to make your peace with that behavior. Or at least you may not react so strongly to it. In other cases, even when you know the cultural explanation for a certain behavior, you may still not like it. Fine. But what have you lost by trying to understand?

Lesson Seven

Most people do behave rationally; you just have to discover the rationale. Foreigners aren't acting this way just to get your goat. This is really how they are. They come by their crazy norms the same way you come by yours: through the process of cultural conditioning described in chapter 1. You may not think much of a particular bit of irritating behavior, but can you really say it isn't legitimate?

This, then, is our story: even though we know better, we all look around us and see not other people, but ourselves. And while we accept, intellectually, that others—especially foreigners—can't possibly be like us, we behave for all the world as if they were. Oddly enough, our experience of the world doesn't always change our understanding of it; that is, our deeply felt notion of how things must be often prevails over our experience of how things are.

In time, however, through encounters like those presented here, we can begin to change our view of ourselves and the world and come to believe that they are not one and the same. Once we have done that, we will truly be citizens of the world.

How to Write a Dialogue

The dialogue concept is a flexible one. It can be used in any kind of training or other setting where the object is to make people aware of how other people are different from them.

For a successful dialogue, there are four ingredients, each of which is discussed below:

1. the conversation must sound natural

2. the difference or mistake must not be obvious

3. the mistake must not be a result of some esoteric knowledge the average reader would never have heard of, and

4. the conversation should contain clues to the difference (which one sees when they are pointed out).

The reader or workshop participant must identify immediately with the conversation; that is, he or she must instinctively feel that this is an entirely believable situation and an entirely likely verbal exchange. In the best dialogues, the reader feels that he or she has in fact *had* this conversation or something very much like it. To compose a good dialogue, then, be sure the situation you set up is believable and the language you use is how people really talk.

The success of this whole technique depends on people reading the dialogue and not seeing anything "wrong." As we noted in chapter 1, if the "mistakes" or cultural differences were obvious, people wouldn't be having conversations like these. The reader must be convinced that these aren't just the sort of things that unaware, insensitive people might say, but that he or she could very easily have made these same remarks. And the only way to make this point is to construct the dialogues in such a way that nothing appears to have happened or to be "wrong" with these remarks. If the reader sees nothing wrong here, then he or she has to admit that: "Yes, I could have said something like this. Anyone could have." When readers think that, you've got them where you want them.

At the same time, the dialogue must not turn on some esoteric bit of information average readers would never have heard of, something to the effect that white is the color of mourning in India or you never wrap wedding presents in red in Paraguay. The readers or workshop participants should feel that if only they were a little more aware, a little more alert, they would have seen the mistake coming and avoided it. But if the mistake hinges on an obscure piece of information, then the reader could only avoid it by sheer coincidence, which means that he or she does not identify with the dialogue and can easily dismiss it as unrealistic. You must never give the reader or trainee an excuse to discount the dialogue.

Finally, the key to the dialogue should be somewhere in it. This is not to say that the explanation for what has gone wrong must be in the dialogue, but there must be some hint or clue which, if the readers could only see it, would tip them off to an impending (or unfolding) misunderstanding or faux pas. This gives them some hope that, with a little practice and a new way of seeing, they might be able to start avoiding such mistakes. If cultural differences can never really be apprehended, then what's the point in knowing about them?

The actual writing of a dialogue is not as hard as all this makes it sound. Most of the dialogues in this book were triggered by a single observation and the first draft written in a few minutes. In most cases, though not all, the process was the same:

1. You think of, or are otherwise made aware of, a particular cultural value or attitude, either American or foreign.

2. You think up a concrete example of a situation where this value or attitude would come into play.

3. You imagine the conversation that would take place in that situation between someone who holds that value and someone who doesn't.

4. You polish and refine the dialogue as necessary to make it more natural, more subtle, a little humorous if possible, and a little surprising.

One of my favorite dialogues is #20, Waiting for the Contract:

MS. WARREN: Is the contract ready then?

MR. CHAO: I'm afraid not. Mr. Sung still hasn't prepared it.

MS. WARREN: He's not very efficient, is he?

MR. CHAO: Not anymore. But he used to be an excellent worker. I've been trying to find out what's wrong.

MS. WARREN: What did he say to you?

This dialogue started life as the perfectly commonplace observation that Americans are very direct. I then thought of a concrete example of directness: asking someone what's bothering him or her. I then located that example in a real-life situation, in this case in a work setting, and imagined the conversation between someone who behaved in that way and someone who didn't. You'll find that the dialogue has all but written itself once you get this far into it.

Sometimes it isn't a value or attitude that occurs to you, but a curious bit of behavior. This was the genesis for Wedding Bells (#17): the notion of arranged marriages, which Americans find difficult to understand.

ALICE: I heard your son is getting married.
        Congratulations.

FATIMA: Thank you. The wedding will be
         next spring.

ALICE: How nice for you. How did they
        meet?

FATIMA: Oh, they haven't actually met yet.

With this difference in behavior as a beginning, it was a short step to imagining the conversation between a person from a culture where people choose their spouse and one from a culture where they don't. Notice here that the conversation isn't about arranged marriages per se—dialogues are never *about* the cultural difference. The difference in marriage customs is revealed in the dialogue. The purpose of a dialogue is to *illustrate* a cultural difference, to render cultural differences into instances of behavior, not to identify or explain those differences.

Another source of material is to think of situations you were in where the unexpected happened or where what you assumed to be the case was not. Then try to think of why this happened, what was behind your expectation or assumption? Once you've identified the norm, it should then be easy to convert the situation into a conversation.

Index of Dialogues by Country/Region

Arab/Middle Eastern

German

Hispanic

Indian

Japanese

Mediterranean

Russian